Not Who
I Pictured

A Phós Publication

ISBN-13: 9780692111567
Library of Congress Control Number: 2018942483

CONTENTS

1.

Hourglass
Jordan Nadler

I often wonder how much of the desire to uncover details about my ancestors is actually about them at all. I have joined the family-history crusaders, nosing around the past, trying to fill in my family tree with personalities behind the names. This was fun, at first, until I realized that a voyage into the past inevitably leads to the present, where memory is supposed to live.

We are told that contentment is found by being in the present. And yet, we are so often seduced by access to the past; as if the lives of our ancestors are somehow untapped parts of us; as if there are people, long gone, sitting in picture frames in our homes who might be able to quell the inevitable existential crises we have when we wonder who, and why, we are who we are, if only we could have known them better.

That is all to say, here is a picture of my great grandmother, Vera Shapiro, in an evening gown on a cruise ship in the middle of the Great Depression.

This photo has been displayed in a small, inconspicuous silver frame in my grandparents' apartment in the Bronx all my life. It has always been a favorite, invoking a feeling of flapper-era nostalgia, next to a stack of hardcover books about F. Scott Fitzgerald and Frank Sinatra. I liked the idea of an ancestor frozen in time as a beautiful, young woman, epitomizing glamour. Somewhere around her on that ship is my great grandfather, her husband, Maurice Shapiro, the facilitator of the voyage, the dress, and a generation of American opulence.

It never occurred to me to find out more than the narrative given to them by my grandmother and father. They were Russian immigrants who met on the ship coming to America at the turn of the twentieth century; elegant, gregarious and wealthy. That was it. There was no context, no life before America, no sign of struggle. Just, Russian and wealthy. Perhaps it was a coincidence, but my curiosity about their lives began to flood through me about the same time that my grandmother began to lose all of her memories. And just like that, my access to our family's past took the shape of an hourglass that had been turned on its head. From an arduous search of historical documents, and a handful of corroborate-able facts from my grandmother, this is the story I am able to tell.

Let's start with the old country.

Maurice Shapiro was born on May 5, 1897 to Sarah Berlinnerblau and a father whose name remains unknown. Records show he was born in Kiev, however my father told me the family had resided in Odessa. Perhaps they moved at some point. Either way, they were Jews in what is now Ukraine at the turn of the twentieth century. Maurice's father died in 1910, when he was thirteen years old. Soon after, his mother, unable to take care of three children on her own, sent him and his older brother, Ilusha, away to Bremen, Germany, possibly to live with an uncle.

Four years later, Maurice, seventeen, and Ilusha boarded the Prince Friedrich Wilhem at the Bremen harbor and sailed to New York. It was on this ship that Maurice serendipitously met Vera Weinstock, who was about fifteen years old, and was immigrating to the States with her very large Russian family.

Vera was one of five sisters and a brother, on board with their parents, Moses and Sarah, and a maternal grandmother. They were sailing away from what I recently found out was an incredibly luxurious, aristocratic life -- one that my father likened to the world of Anna Karenina. Moses had been the owner of a substantial brewery which he ran until the Czar and the Cossaks made Jews' lives untenable. Vera's childhood had been one of servants, governesses, a seamstress, laundress, cook and personal horse-and-carriage. But by 1914, the splendor of their lives was, as described by my father, "eviscerated by anti-semitism." Moses put his brewery in the name of a foreman, bought eight one-way tickets to America and left everything else behind. The Weinstocks would never

4

regain their wealth, nor would they ever return to Russia, a country for which, by the end, there was no love lost.

And so on it was on that ship Vera met Maurice, and the ocean lulled away the titles, social structures and class systems of the past. They were teenagers in love, and the American Dream was the great equalizer. They arrived in New York around May 21, 1914, almost two months to the day before the beginning of World War One -- a war in which the country Maurice had been living for the last four years brutally battled against the country he was from; the country in which his mother and brother were still living, a homeland he, too, would never see again.

*

America

In 1920, census records show Maurice and Vera, twenty two and nineteen years old respectively, were living with her parents and two of her sisters, twenty one year old Ray and seventeen year old Pauline, in Brooklyn. Maurice was listed as a salesman at a leather-coat factory. Moses was now a dealer at a vegetable store. Though Vera and her mother were not working, her sister, Ray, was an operator at a waste factory, and Pauline, a correspondent-clerk at a watch office. The First World War had ended two years prior, and the country they had all left was in the hands of the Bolsheviks. The Russian Empire was now the Soviet Union.

Regardless, my ancestors were living in New York, working ordinary jobs, living unremarkable lives. I imagine at this point they had all begun to learn English. Though, decades after this census was taken, my father's most prominent memories of his grandmother and four great aunts are still all of them sitting in various living rooms together, playing cards and yelling at each other in Russian.

Maurice at this point seemed to be keeping his head down and working for a wage. He was newly married and living with his in-laws. Around this time, their son, Isador, (or Edward) was born. Five years later, in 1925, Maurice signed a Declaration of Intention to become an American citizen, and in 1928 he signed the official petition for naturalization. He was now thirty one years old, and though still listed as a salesman, he and Vera had moved out of her parents' home and were living at 179 Ocean Parkway in Brooklyn. Two years later, the 1930 census shows them in a new apartment on the same street. Vera was most likely pregnant with my grandmother, Barbara, and they had a live-in servant named Sarah Brolly from Northern Ireland. Maurice was now listed as a business broker. It was within a couple years of this census that the photo of Vera on the cruise was taken.

*

The Big Time

Families like to pinpoint ancestors who "started it all," and use their lives and accomplishments as a foundation for parts of their own identities. As it pertains to my father's side, those people have always been Maurice and Vera. But their stories have always skipped straight over the first decade-and-a-half of their assimilation and early lives in New York, and landed, instead, in the middle of their success, as if Maurice and Vera stepped off the Prince Friedrich Wilhelm on Ellis Island and boarded a cruise to Bermuda; as if their lives were not also greatly shaped by those who came before them.

In reality, Maurice, with Vera by his side, arrived in New York City at seventeen years old, and carved a lavish life for his family out of immigrant clay. Their lifestyle had nothing to do with the wealth the Weinstocks had once upon a time, as that wealth no longer existed. He came to America with nothing, but within a little more than a decade, had created enough prosperity that it took nearly one hundred years before any one of his ancestors stopped and asked how he did it at a time when most of the country had been brought to its knees. His business was in mergers and acquisitions. He apparently had a knack for it, but kept his name out of the newspapers. While poverty-stricken men jumped to their deaths from rooftops, Maurice and Vera were at the opera. I can't imagine they were ambivalent or unempathetic to the plights of those around them, but objectively, they were unaffected.

Though Jewish, Maurice and Vera were not at all religious, and did not Bar or Bat Mitzvah either of their children. Though Vera only had an eighth grade education, and Maurice a high school education, they were apparently incredibly well read, well traveled and well manicured. They seemed to have skipped over much of the harsh assimilation endured by other Jewish immigrants. The most "Jewish" thing they did in New York was move to the Upper West Side in the 1940s.

No one in my family ever questioned how or why our patriarch just seemed to side-step the Great Depression like it was a puddle on the street. But I've come to learn, in bits and pieces, that Maurice did not do so easily. He just did so quietly. And if the devil is in the detail, then he has left a bit of a frustratingly angelic story behind. The memories have run out. The questions should have been asked years ago. The only reference in the *Brooklyn Eagle* to a Maurice Shapiro that appeared to be about him was a brief mention of a linen store being sold and bought.

What I was able to surmise is that he put his name on little, but fingerprints on much, and left traces of himself around institutions in New York City and beyond. He was, I have been told but cannot confirm, a couple of degrees of separation away from the invention of the Moscow Mule (after merging Smirnoff vodka with Heublein), as well as the chairman of the board of Seagrave, the largest fire truck company in the United States, which is based in Wisconsin. My father, aunt and grandmother told me that there were hundreds of deals he facilitated, but few for which he sought notoriety. There is an absence of documentation as to how he made his money -- not a word in countless public records, newspapers, scholarly journals, historical documents, or histories of New York. That, combined with my grandmother's fading memory, my father's lack of knowledge about his grandfather's business deals, and the fact that -- other than a Russian faction of our family who stayed in the old country before World War I and changed their names, making them untraceable -- led to a dead end. There are only a handful of living people in this world who knew my great grandparents, and their shared bloodline has done nothing to change the fact that at some point, my entire extended family lost touch with each other.

*

It so dumbly failed to occur to me that memories can die before the people harboring them do. Even as I held my grandfather's hand as he slipped away six years ago, having battled Alzheimer's for a decade, it just didn't occur to me to document the intricacies of the answers I was given about our family's past; to dig deeper, and find out more. I always thought I should film my grandmother giving an account of her upbringing, to have as a keepsake. But I intended for the footage to be a memento, not the vault and key.

At the end of the day, I waited too long. Is it enough that their blood courses through my veins? Here is a photo of my great grandmother in an evening gown on a cruise during the Great Depression. She and Maurice are the earliest ancestors I will ever be able to see simply because there are no photographs of their parents; at least none I have ever seen. My grandmother is the oldest relative I will have loved, heard and touched. If I have children, technology will allow them to see her and hear her voice. I guess what's maddening is the color I will have to relinquish; that I will have to accept the memories I'm seeking are trapped in a mind that has lost access to them.

"I can't remember what I know," my grandmother said shaking her head, frustrated when she couldn't find anything to tell me about her childhood one day. It wasn't that she didn't know the facts anymore, she just couldn't get to them. She did remember that Vera won the prize for best-dressed woman on the cruise where this photograph was taken, which would not have been surprising since all of her clothes were back to being handmade.

So here I am in 2018, one hundred and four years after Maurice and Vera met on a ship, wishing I could fill in the blanks, wondering what it would even change if I could. I never knew my great grandparents, but in some way it feels like they're dying again. Pre-maturely, even. As my grandmother's memories decline, the photo seems to fade.

With my grandmother's story goes so many others'. As her life inches towards its end, and as the person she was flickers in and out of her with growing intensity, goes entire generations of people I will most likely never be able to know or understand in any better capacity. People who had long, full lives; people who fled wars, who lived through them, who prospered on foreign shores; people who died young, who lost their children, who changed their identities to survive. People, like Maurice's mother, who apparently loved music -- and that one fact is all that can be summed up about her entire existence a few generations later.

This is a photo of a woman who sometimes resembles me, who died a long time ago when her heart stopped beating, and is leaving us once more as memories of her disappear.

2.

An Insignificant Man
Linh P. Nguyen

I discovered the photograph of my Great Uncle Tham Hoang Tin after I asked to see one of my great grandmother. I had seen the photo on her tombstone in a cemetery on the outskirts of Hanoi. She was strikingly beautiful and I wanted to see if my family had another copy. I was with my parents at my grandmother's home and when she returned with the photo I wanted, I began to ask about her mother and our family. That is when my grandmother mentioned in passing she had an uncle whose position, I later came to believe, could have placed the family in great jeopardy.

My grandmother -- who like all of my grandparents, fought for the Communist North in the war against the Americans -- told me her family had been a wealthy one, and that she herself had studied in private French schools in the years when Vietnam was still a French colony. But of all her relatives, none was more important than her Uncle Tin. Trained as a pharmacist, he had entered politics and in 1950 became mayor of Hanoi. He served for two years. More specifically, he served as a functionary in the colonial government. Two years after his term ended, the French were defeated at Dien Bien Phu and the Communists took control of Hanoi.

Many who had served the French were "encouraged" to go to re-education camps, so that they would learn Ho Chi Minh's governing philosophy, and rid themselves of the vestiges of colonialism.

This sounded ominous. Which made me wonder, what happened to Uncle Tin?

*

On the morning of October 10, 1954, five thousand

communist soldiers, also known as the *Vietminh*, paraded through the center of Hanoi, claiming a full takeover of their capital city. Finally, after nine years of war with the French, Hanoi belonged to the Vietnamese once again. Hundreds of thousands of people could be seen crying, cheering and singing on the streets. The celebration went on for two hours. New flags were unfurled -- red flags with a yellow star. The French had withdrawn after nearly a century of colonial rule.

Somewhere in the city, my Uncle Tin was speaking to two other men in a small office. They were captured in this photograph, Tin sitting on the far right. No one knows what they were discussing. He was forty five years old and, I assumed, doomed.

He was born in 1909, four years before imperial Vietnam welcomed its last emperor. As if one thousand years of Chinese occupation prior to that wasn't enough, the country was in the midst of the French rule. Most of the population was living in poverty, struggling to adjust to the new ways of their new Western masters. Only a small fraction of the people thrived in the new regime. They spoke fluent French, attended French schools, had maids at home and dressed like their Western counterparts. They were hated by most of their fellow citizens, seen as the "bourgeoisie" who followed the white men. My family was among them.

Tin dressed as a Westerner. He spoke fluent French and had a mustache like that of Clark Gable in *Gone With the Wind*. In 1932, he left his first wife and went to Paris to study to become a pharmacist. After finishing his degree, he returned to Hanoi and opened his own pharmacy. He married twice more; his wives died of illness, or were killed when war came to Vietnam.

The French appointed forty six mayors of Hanoi but it was not until 1945 -- after the defeat of the Japanese and around the time of independence -- that they appointed a Vietnamese. Uncle Tin was the second-to-last mayor of Hanoi the French appointed. Because he was neither the first, nor the last, nor, I would learn, the most distinguished, his name is all but absent from histories of that time.

Still, he is credited with a few accomplishments: the

renovation of the The Huc Bridge across the most historically important lake in central Hanoi; and a seemingly innocuous, but potentially grievous error. There is a garden in a central square in Hanoi that the French called Rond Point Puginier. In 1945, as the independence movement grew, someone renamed it Garden of Independence. But when Uncle Tin took office, mindful of who he served, he gave it a new name, presumably more acceptable to the French – Hong Bang Garden, referring to a Vietnamese dynasty in the twenty ninth century B.C. He just had to pick a name *that* ancient.

One might say, from a patriot's perspective, he was not on his country's side. He benefited from the colonizer's regime, lived a comfortable life, and helped rule the capital city. One might say he was not especially noble, or so I thought. But when fighting worsened between the French and Vietminh, he sent medical supplies to his countrymen.

*

In the summer of 1954, Vietnam and France came together in Geneva to sign a peace accord, ending their brutal, almost decade-long war. The country was now temporarily divided at the Seventeenth Parallel into North and South Vietnam.

In the following months, close to one million northern Vietnamese migrated to the South to flee the Communist government in what the U.S. Navy called the "Operation Passage to Freedom." There were also many who stayed behind, whether by choice or force, including my Uncle Tin. But in October 1954, his protectors were gone. I look at the photograph and wonder if he was awaiting his fate in that room.

*

Uncle Tin left virtually no footprint. I searched for him in books and databases, both in English and Vietnamese. I found a brief mention in a Wikipedia page but that told me very little. I did know, however, when he died -- in 1991, in

Paris. He would have been eighty two years old. He had survived. But how?

I sought out a scholar, John D. Phan, hoping he might know where I could look. Phan, who is Vietnamese-American, teaches at Columbia University. As it turns out, his family was among those who fled the North in 1954.

He never heard of my great uncle but did offer some resources that led to a clue. The Communists, I found out, wanted the support of the people and knew they might secure this by making use of those who had served the French, or the "intellectuals." But not before they were deemed ready.

Tin had several children, including a son, Tham Vu Can. He splits his time between Paris and Hanoi, and that was where I found him, with my grandmother's help.

I had several questions for him, but the only thing he told me was that he and his brother, Long, had written some articles about his father, and he'd send them to me. Beyond that, though we were cousins, he was reluctant to talk.

The articles were personal and very flattering. He described his father as a patriotic man, who despite being a beneficiary of the French rule, did all he could to help his people. And lest anyone doubt his commitment to the North, he wrote that shortly before the Communists took power, his father was evacuated to the "fire-free" zone, along with his wife and they were "encouraged" to return to Hanoi to help rebuild the city and the country. I write "encouraged" because, while the article says so explicitly, I cannot help but wonder if he was first sent to a re-education camp.

Tin was not the only pharmacist nor former mayor brought back to the capital. He was appointed head of the research laboratory in Viet Duc Hospital, the biggest hospital at the time in Hanoi. His son said, despite being an official in the old government, Tin was respected by the Communist party for his loyalty to serving the country and as an intellectual in the medical field.

I found this odd. If Tin was well respected by the French government, wouldn't the Communists want to get rid of him soon after they took over the country? I did an Internet search on the mayor after Uncle Tin, the last appointed by the French, Do Quang Giai, and found a story from 1954 about him in *The New York Times*. The Communists had fired him after learning he had accepted French aid to evacuate anti-Communist civilians from the Red River delta. "Mayor Do Quang Giai," the story read, "had been actively cooperating with the French in a plan to take out all who wanted to leave."

He was replaced by an anti-French official, fled to the South with his family, went into business, became chairman of the Vietnam British Association and received an honorary medal of the Order of the British Empire (OBE). He then worked for the U.S. Embassy in Vietnam. He was known for his opposition to the North Vietnamese government and supported President Nixon's policy in Vietnam. There's no information about what happened to him after the war ended.

Meanwhile, Uncle Tin continued working at the hospital, and for all intents and purposes kept his head down. As a former mayor under the country's "enemy" regime, his story is remarkably undramatic. But perhaps that's why the Communists kept him around. He posed no threat. He was useful.

And it paid off in the end. My great uncle lived to witness the country reunify in 1975, after the Vietnam War, which the Vietnamese call the American War. At some point, he was granted permission to leave Vietnam to go to France to receive medical treatment. He had relatives living in Paris. Among them were his children, who were with him when he died.

3.

An Escape to Hell
Chloe Picchio

My grandfather wanted to be a soldier but he was too young, so his brother Peter helped him. Peter took his birth certificate and smudged the birth date, making my grandfather eighteen, two years older than he really was. The army accepted the ruse and my grandfather got what he so badly wanted: a one-way ticket out of his dead-end town via the 109th Infantry Regiment of the United States Army. It was 1939 and still peace time. My grandfather thought he had found a way out of hell; an escape from Pennsylvania's coal fields where the anthracite earth swallowed men whole and set houses ablaze. But then the war came and he never quite came back.

He only existed in my life through a series of snapshots. I saw Luciano Picchio, my grandfather, cautiously looking over his shoulder as he cut his wedding cake, beaming at my infant father and grandmother in their first family Christmas picture, and wearing *Gone With the Wind*-esque suspenders next to my grandmother in a hoop skirt during Scranton's centennial celebration. Behind his broad smile and a baby face my father and I shared, I sensed a sadness or tiredness. I always assumed this came from what my father described as a "hardscrabble childhood," first faced by my grandfather, and then my father and his siblings. But neither he, nor my father and his brother or sister ever complained. It wasn't the coal region's way. Whining was reserved as a luxury for the rich, who had the time and money to ruminate. Everyone else just dusted themselves off and moved on. Moving on meant burying the past, something which cut me off from the unpleasantness in my grandfather's and father's lives. What little I did know was that my grandfather and his nine siblings grew up stuffed into a little house on 536 East Grant Street in Olyphant, Pennsylvania.

Then as it still is now, Olyphant's notoriety was tied to the bleak fact that it had the most bars per capita in the state. Its residents needed the distraction since they lived lives that barely skimmed the surface. The coal companies held mineral rights to the land under the homes, meaning that many of the immigrants who sought the American dream in their hard-earned craftsman cottages never truly owned anything. Scranton Coal Company and the Lackawanna Iron & Coal Company possessed those dreams instead. Their currency was anthracite coal, a fuel with the highest energy density that made it perfect for heating large factories. Sitting on the northern tip of Appalachia, the Pennsylvania coal region served as the industry's beating heart. Small towns like Olyphant were its veins, with plentiful nuggets of coal spilling out of the ground like bloody cuts. The cheap workforce of Southern and Eastern Europeans kept the furnaces running for industrial cities throughout the Northeast, as the coal companies funneled their product into a spine of railroads stretching from Buffalo to Boston.

Scranton, the county seat, soon became a symbol of the early twentieth century's hunger for wealth, like a character from the "Great Gatsby" who couldn't spend their riches quickly enough. It was known as the "Electric City," earning its nickname through the first-ever electric streetcars rolling down the avenues leading to an exotic menagerie of elephants and tigers at the local zoo. Five miles away, in Olyphant, those luxuries seemed like distant fantasies. Mining, even a generation removed from the underage breaker boys who were crushed to death under their coal carts, was dangerous. Anthracite mining required more blasting and deeper tunnels than those for bituminous coal, creating fragile coal seams where any small mistake became amplified with grave consequences. Explosions happened regularly, ignited by a little spark from a miner's lamp or pipe. Hundreds of men died the year of my grandfather's birth; their deaths by suffocation and gas explosion distilled into insurance company columns focusing on issues of liability and fault. This was all for $7.53 a day. The miners existed precariously at the bottom rung of the middle class, one workplace injury away from financial ruin. Still, it was enough to feed a family in the midst of the Depression, and the abundance of the coal fields was an exception in a country filled with homelessness and dust storms. Everyone in town worked in the mines whether they liked it or not. The earth underneath Olyphant's main streets would occasionally buckle, the reverberations of a mining accident bubbling towards the surface, engulfing a home, a car, or a dream. My grandfather refused to be pulled underground with them. He wanted more.

"More" manifested itself as it always has for young men from poor families without many academic prospects, in either professional sports or the military. Professional sports were a pipe dream; my grandfather's lanky six-foot frame made him look like a "decent" baseball player but without the skill set or access to training to become "great." That left him with one choice, the army. There were far worse options; it certainly was a step up from the mines where his father's lungs filled with coal dust. The military offered far more intrigue than tending sheep, the default family option for centuries back in the mountains of central Italy. My grandfather wasn't alone in his desire to leave. He joined an ever-increasing stream of people filtering out of the Scranton area in 1930 that has continued until today. So, on October 30, 1939, he packed his backpack, closed his locker at Olyphant High School, and went off to the army recruitment office, doctored birth certificate in hand.

No one knows for sure why my grandfather left. It was probably for the money, but it could have been influenced by patriotism or a naive sense of adventure. In his regimental portrait taken two years later, in the spring of 1941, he's holding a small white dog, looking more like Tintin and Snowy ready to spy on the Soviets than a man about to go to war. Maybe like Tintin, my grandfather thought things would be easier than they ultimately were; that they would have a storybook ending where he came out on top. He loved to hunt. He might have thought the war would be similar to the animalistic adrenaline he felt when felling a six-point buck. I doubt he was ready to hunt people. But in a few short months, that's what he would be expected to do.

I always felt like my grandfather's military service was an enigma. Throughout my childhood, it came in flashes: a brief viewing of his Purple Heart on Veteran's Day or in the expensive patriotic floral arrangements my grandmother ordered without fail for his shelf in the mausoleum each Memorial Day. No one ever talked about what he actually saw in the war because he rarely spoke about it. Information dripped out like a leaky faucet, the discoveries infrequent but telling. Homemade jug wine prompted my great uncles to divulge that my grandfather had been in D-Day, painting a dramatic picture of how he stormed the beaches of Normandy, rivaling the opening sequence of *Saving Private Ryan*. That glory was tainted with awkwardness as they chuckled about how my grandfather had lied about his age, was caught, sent back to finish high school, and promptly returned to the army. Yet no one questioned his choice. Anyone who witnessed my grandfather's decision is now either dead or ill. But in the end, it doesn't matter. What matters is what he saw and could never unsee.

America's war began with Pearl Harbor on December 7, 1941, but my grandfather's war began eleven months earlier on February 17, 1941. Despite President Roosevelt's lip service to isolationist policies that would keep America out of the war, he also knew the truth. After France fell to the Germans in 1940, military advisors built up National Guard units, like my grandfather's, in anticipation of a global conflict. Although they had been training for months, their first destination wasn't the beaches of Europe, but the swamps of Camp Livingston, Louisiana. In a cheerful little diary decorated with a happy cartoon soldier, he dutifully noted that they woke up each morning at 4:30, generally ate lunch around noon, and were free after 8 p.m. This monotonous routine continued for months, as they went to training camps throughout the South in preparation for what would soon be known as the invasion of France. On October 8, 1943 the 109th Infantry Regiment shipped off to England as a part of the larger 28th Infantry Division under General Omar Bradley.

My grandfather wasn't at D-Day. That exaggeration began like most family myths, where time extends and combines threads of truth to identify with famous events. He actually arrived in France two months later with his regiment as a part of Operation Cobra. Operation Cobra served as the second wave of troops, helping to relieve those too tired or injured to carry on throughout the little seaside towns of France with the hope of pushing towards Paris. Sometimes entire battles only covered a quarter of a mile. The troops were wedged into a twenty mile long pocket, roughly the length of Manhattan, and surrounded on all sides. Inching towards the capitol took its toll. Both the Allied and German troops together suffered one hundred thousand casualties during the campaign.

The few observations my grandfather passed down focused not on the carnage, but were the mundane observations of a teenager. He hated both the British and the French. The French were too effeminate, and the fact that this was the second time Americans rescued their country from Germany irked him. British troops were less annoying, though their constant tea-times slowed the troops' already snail's pace of progress. At some point in the foothills of France, that slow trudge towards Paris left my grandfather time to get in trouble, too. He was demoted from sergeant to private, a drop of five pay-grades. The reason why is locked in some dusty cabinet or held up in red tape deep within the National Archives in St. Louis. My grandfather could have had a youthful bar brawl, a fight in camp, or worse. But his real moment of terror was still to come.

Saint-Sever-Calvados is a footnote in most World War II history books, just another burned-out French village taken by the Allies in the latter half of Operation Cobra. Its most notable attribute is the famous fourteenth-century miniature *The Deluge*, a part of a series of small paintings depicting the Apocalypse. On blood-red hills men and horses writhe in agony, falling into the earth towards Hell. The misproportioned men fold over into unfathomable positions, stretching in vain towards the earth's surface. At the time of its creation, these figures could have been reaching for salvation in the midst of a bloody crusade or begging for death to ease the suffering of the plague. What the painters didn't know was that it would happen six hundred years later in August, 1944.

A stalemate dragged on for eight days in the early August heat, with the Allied forces pinned at the bottom of the hill against the well-stocked German artillery. On the ninth day of fighting, my grandfather led troops towards the German position at the crest of the hill. A fifty-millimeter shell exploded in front of him, ripping shrapnel through his legs and back, leaving a chunk of his calf on the battlefield. Little did he know he would never be whole again. My grandfather was soon transported to a military hospital in England, where he received a Purple Heart along with the two other injured men in his unit. To the outside world, he was a hero, worthy of front page coverage.

"Private Picchio is improving rapidly and will soon return to duty," the hospital ward officer First Lieutenant James Mood said to the Mid-Valley Gazette, a local Olyphant paper.

That was a lie.

My grandfather would never fully recover. His physical wounds would heal, but his mind would forever be scarred. During his time in the English hospital, a female psychiatrist told my grandfather that he was exhibiting signs of shell shock, better known now as post-traumatic stress disorder. She suggested he get treatment; he refused. My grandfather's decision was rooted in shame and a century-long misunderstanding of the condition.

First recognized in World War I, where the brutality of trench warfare made men shake uncontrollably, shell shock, as it was then known, was tied to cowardice. Men who had it were perceived as "lesser," shirking duty, unlike their tougher counterparts. By the middle of World War II, Army physicians determined that it was tied to combat as 1.4 million men had been diagnosed with the condition. Yet, the best treatment they offered was sodium pentathol as a temporary sedative and rest, before the soldiers were sent back to the front. Preliminary studies from the time of my grandfather's injury mentioned that shell shock must be connected to the number of days spent in combat. Army doctors argued that anything over ninety days in combat would result in a psychiatric breakdown. His unit saw 196.

Although his war should have been over, my grandfather was thrown back into action. His unit marched down the wide Champs-Élysées on August 29, marking the beginning of victory in Europe. But all was not well in the 109th. Of the twenty one thousand men charged with desertion during the war, only one, Eddie Slovik, a draftee from Michigan, was executed. Slovik's troubles began in October of 1944 when he requested to be transferred from a front line position to another one in the rear. When his superiors refused, he decided to leave his post and go to a French military hospital.

"They were shelling the town, and we were told to dig in for the night. The following morning they were shelling us again," Slovik wrote in a note confessing his desertion. "I was so scared, nerves and trembling, that at the time the other replacements moved out, I couldn't move. I stayed there in my foxhole til it was quiet and I was able to move. I then walked into town. I said that I had to go out there again I'd run away. He said there was nothing he could do for me so I ran away again AND I'LL RUN AWAY AGAIN IF I HAVE TO GO OUT THERE."

After six weeks with a Canadian military unit, Slovik walked back into camp. He wrote his confession, and after declining several offers to retract his statement and go back to his unit, he went before a court-martial. Slovik thought, as he had seen in other cases, that his court-martial would only result in jail time. He was wrong. Desertion was a systemic problem on the French front, and someone needed to be the scapegoat. On January 31, 1945 at 10:04 a.m. stripped of all his clothing save a regulation blanket to keep out the cold, Eddie Slovik was shot by a firing squad of twelve men. They didn't shoot to kill; it took fifteen minutes.

Eddie Slovik and my grandfather were interchangeable. They were both working-class young men from ethnic communities who ended up marrying women named Antoinette. More importantly, they were both scared. It's just that my grandfather was better at hiding it.

The 109th, as a part of the larger 28th, fought in the Battle of Hürtgen Forest, the longest foreign battle the army ever fought. My grandfather's unit was the first to pierce

German defenses and reach enemy soil, running through what were called "dragon teeth," the pyramid shaped spikes meant to impale tanks and trap men. Those teeth, cynically called "pimples" by Allied troops, fortified the seemingly impenetrable Siegfried Line, a retrenchment of World War I tunnels with the addition of eighteen thousand bunkers, tunnels, and tank traps. My grandfather's unit was lucky to make it through the defenses unscathed. Most of the battle, however, was spent as sitting ducks, with the American forces unprepared to fight through the dense forest, and ill-equipped for the starvation and cold of winter. Twenty four thousand Americans died, marking it as one of the biggest military failures in American history.

Yet my grandfather somehow survived. He arrived in Germany, marveling at the cleanliness of the houses and the technology in the kitchens of the homes the regiment occupied. I still have fragments documenting his time there; a large silver ring depicting a crudely carved llama, which had been handed to him by a German prisoner of war who had been a metalsmith, and a copy of *Life* magazine, in which he supposedly is one of the nameless GIs shown with their backs towards the camera running towards action. In November 1945, he gave his last salute when the division was disbanded in Harrisburg, Pennsylvania and went back to his old life.

*

While the war raged on, Scranton stood still. The coal furnaces burned faster than ever to meet the increased demands for fuel, but the poverty in coal mining families stayed the same. The little house in Olyphant my grandfather returned to in November 1945 was also exactly the same as he had left it, with one exception. Flush with cash for the first time ever, my grandfather wanted to gift his family the trappings of domesticity his parents could never afford. That December he bought his family's first Christmas tree, with yards of lights and store-bought ornaments. For a brief moment, the possibilities for my grandfather's future shined as brightly as the decorations in their window. Like many of the other returning men, he could have used the money to go to college on the GI Bill, which brought thousands of veterans into the middle class and ushered in the prosperity of the 1950s. Others saved the money to start businesses or purchase homes. But not my grandfather.

A couple weeks later, his family dropped a bomb, explosive as anything that fell during the war. Years of unpaid taxes meant that the family would lose their home, and the mounting lien threatened the shame of an inevitable sheriff's sale. For my grandfather, the thought of a Penn State education was nice, but family honor meant everything. His brothers refused to divide the cost, spending their own money somewhere else. Alone, my grandfather took on the burden of shoring up the family finances. What he didn't know was that he had locked himself into thirty years of struggle, where he barely managed to scrape by.

Love, or the promise of love, pays little attention to convenient timing or financial stability. My grandparents thought they found love in a carpool to the Billig Shoe Factory in Archbald, Pennsylvania. It was a carpool romance; my grandmother Antoinette Iammangini, who worked in the secretarial pool, disliked and rebuffed the overtures of my grandfather, a machine worker who drove her to work everyday. At some point, annoyance must have turned into affection, and they were married. They were an attractive match made in superficial heaven. To my grandmother who always mimicked one of her numerous silver screen idols, Scarlett O'Hara, my grandfather must have been Rhett Butler, a war hero, dark, and adventurous. There wasn't an Ashley Wilkes that got away, only lost opportunities of college and grandeur, like my grandfather's. In her, he saw Scarlett's crackling wit and nineteen-inch waist. Their wedding on June 10, 1950 meant that at twenty seven, my grandfather was finally an adult in Italian culture--no longer tied to his family. He finally left Olyphant and moved four miles away.

Life improved in the wide craftsman-style house on 366 Main Street in Archbald. My grandmother boasted to everyone within earshot that the deed included the mineral rights to the home, meaning that no mining company could claim whatever was under the house. Her father laughed, reminding her that the piece of paper meant nothing and the mines ran beneath everything. But no one could spoil her middle class victory. Children came quickly and expensively, my father's birth cost $76 followed by his brother Daniel's two years later, and his sister Marialana's ten years after that. Their births pushed my grandmother further into her game of keeping up with the Joneses. She yearned for the latest appliance or gadget that would mark them as "better," not just the children of immigrants living miles from where their parents settled in America. Throughout my father's childhood he received frivolous gifts like golf clubs and skis inspired by the television version of the Anglo-Saxon upwardly mobile family that they weren't. Eventually, she asked my grandfather to paint their house a bubblegum pink as well as their Plymouth in Pompano Peach, the salmon-y Pantone color of the year. My grandmother, as always, succeeded.

Behind the plastic pink exterior, things were difficult. All that postwar commercialism cost money; money they didn't have. In his various jobs at the Tobyhanna Army Depot and as a bartender at the Italian-American club, my grandfather only made $13,000 a year. My grandmother worked hard as well, but she often spent money as fast as she made it. Still, my grandmother felt successful, quickly rising through the ranks to outearn my grandfather as the head bookkeeper of Carbondale General Hospital. He, on the other hand, drew inward. My grandfather became a shadow of himself, the boy full of adventure lost forever. In its place was an unending monotony, where he worked ten hours a day, went home, and did the same thing again without fail for forty years.

"But better die than live mechanically a life that is a repetition of repetitions," my father said, quoting D.H. Lawrence's book "Women in Love."

That was a book my grandfather would never pick up. Twentieth century English writers were the domain of his three children, who were afforded the benefits of a Jesuit education and went to college through the urging of my grandmother. As with most things, my grandfather stayed silent, neither approving nor disapproving. But his anger constantly simmered beneath the surface.

Sometimes he couldn't take it anymore. It's not clear what triggered him, since post-traumatic stress disorder could be triggered by a sound, a smell, or a phrase that thrust him back into the heat of battle. His anger could have been from other things. Maybe he felt insecure about my grandmother being the primary breadwinner, depriving him of the ability to do what he felt was honorable. Ultimately just like the spark from a miner's pipe that made the mine a tinderbox, the rush of anger came all at once. And it was explosive.

Holidays or Sunday dinners could easily become a war zone. Their kitchen was like the beaches of Normandy, with pots and slaps flying instead of bullets and shrapnel. My grandmother hurled insults across the room, saying that my grandfather was crazy and should have been locked up. Their fights often reached a stalemate. That moment typically came when my grandfather pulled out his hunting rifle and my grandmother her knife. Unless it was one of the few instances where the police were called it ended in rapprochement; mutually assured destruction was averted, until next time. My grandfather retreated to his hunting buddies or the bar, my father retreated to books, eventually becoming a psychiatrist, and my grandmother retreated to *The Guiding Light*.

My grandmother was always afraid of reality. She clung to narratives that could only exist within a television program and held everyone around her to high, fictionalized standards. For her, the soap opera *The Guiding Light* served as an alternate universe, that though full of drama, illustrated the upward mobility she craved. While the convoluted plotlines of the show during the 1950s included an out of wedlock pregnancy and murder, violence was contained within a brief fifteen minutes and inside the safety of a television screen. My grandmother cast herself as Bert Bauer, the hard-driving matriarch of the central family. Bert, like my grandmother, spent extravagantly, living far beyond her means. Bill Bauer, Bert's husband, was the same as my grandfather, a man who was propped up to success by

31

others while his own dreams were set aside. Bert's sons were a doctor and a lawyer. Twenty years later, my grandmother got her doctor and lawyer.

Ultimately, with age, tempers mellowed and things improved. During the 1970s, my grandparents managed to achieve that soap opera quality of life, digging a pool into the backyard despite it being far too cold for much meaningful swimming. My aunt's childhood granted my grandfather a second chance at parenting; he identified more with her sporty resilience than my father's and uncle's bookish natures. They were finally the family my grandmother so desperately wanted from television. But it wouldn't last.

One day, the body that had been shot through and burdened with the concerns of many, finally gave out. My grandfather first felt a weakness in his left side and his strong frame, hardened through years of hunting, began to droop. It was Amyotrophic Lateral Sclerosis, better known as ALS or Lou Gehrig's disease. There is speculation, and some scientific belief, that it might have been caused by the shrapnel, which was spattered throughout his legs and back, suspiciously close to his spinal cord. The disease takes control of people and robs them from the inside out as muscles spasm and die, rendering the patient unable to go to the bathroom, eat, or speak. My grandfather wanted none of it. For a man who was often tied to duty, be it to his family or the army, he wanted to die on his own terms. On July 19, 1985, he declined the use of a respirator, choosing instead to die naturally rather than live artificially. He had lived a life that was a repetition of repetitions.

And then he died, free.

4.

Who She Might Have Been
Deanna Hirsch

I f her mother hadn't died when she was six, the family would have stayed in Paris. She would have been raised a proper French girl and married a proper French boy, perhaps the one standing next to her in the photo – not Jack. She'd have gone to a université instead of Becker Junior College and been a teacher or a journalist, not a travel agent. If Marie had lived Suzanne would have become a mère, not a mom, and taken her babies for walks along the Rue de la Roquette rather than Empire Boulevard. They would've grown up in The City of Light instead of the town of Orangeburg. If her mother hadn't died when she was six there'd be no Mari, named in her memory, no Stephen and no David. And if David hadn't been born where would I be now?

I would not be telling this story about his mother. I would not have set out to learn all I could about a woman who is not my own mother, and whom I met when I was only twenty-three. I talk with my mother-in-law, Suzanne, several times a week, and if I haven't heard from her in a few days I think, "I need to call Suzanne." Over the years I have heard the stories of her growing up, but there is a difference between hearing stories at twenty-three and then again at forty, when you find yourself asking how you end up becoming the person you are. How had Suzanne come to be the person she was, despite all that she had endured? Who was she really before I met her?

Suzanne and Jack live in a two-bedroom townhouse whose walls are covered with photographs – scores of pictures of children and grandchildren and relatives long gone. And then there is one that is tucked between books and trinkets on a cluttered shelf and framed in mahogany. It is the photograph she saved, the rare image of her as a child, when life was simple.

The photo was taken in 1944, around the time that she and her family moved back into their apartment in Paris. The war wasn't yet over but the Germans had left France so the family felt safe to come home. It seems an odd time to pose for a portrait but perhaps when you've been on the run from the Nazis any opportunity for normal, you take. Suzanne doesn't know what they did before the photo was taken or if they had ice cream after. She assumes that her mother was just doing what mothers do, dressing up their kids and capturing memories. Ones that had nothing to do with war.

In the photo, she looks like such a quintessential little girl, from the big bow on top of her head to the teddy bear on her lap. She seems well cared for in an outfit her mother picked out, down to the ankle socks and polished shoes. Her dress is sweet but her expression is stone as she sits on the small wooden chair next to the boy. He's smartly dressed as well, in a sweater, shorts and knee socks, his blond curls creating a soft halo around his head. I always assumed he was her brother. It turns out it was George, her boyfriend.

George and his family lived across the street from her family in Paris. Their school was at the end of the block and like any good boyfriend, she imagines he carried her books to and from. About fifteen years ago, George's sister told her sister that he wanted to see Suzanne when she came back to visit. She happily agreed. They met at restaurant, drank lots of champagne and that was that. Though his face was still pleasant his curls were long gone. He no longer looked like his picture, but then again at sixty-four, neither did she. The only thing the visit stirred up were thoughts of what could have been, not for her and George but for her family.

Suzanne was born in Paris on August 4,1939 to Miriam and Eli Goldberg shortly before the start of World War II. Miriam went by Marie and Eli went by Simon and theirs was a love story of soap operatic proportions. He was a barber. She sold purses and told fortunes on the side. I often wonder how much Marie could tell of her own. The story goes that she was married to a man Suzanne only recalls as "Rosenfeld" and was pregnant with his child when she and Simon met. Simon was so enamored by Marie that he declared, "I'm going to marry her." A few years after Marie gave birth to Estelle, she and Rosenfeld divorced and Simon kept his promise. They married and had Edmond six years after Estelle and Suzanne six years after that.

In 1938, a year before Suzanne was born, Simon's Aunt Betty and her husband Solomon came to France for a visit. The couple lived in Worcester, Massachusetts and sensing that trouble was coming for those with names like Goldberg they offered to sponsor Simon and his family to come to the States. But Marie's ex-husband Rosenfeld refused to let Estelle leave; he had placed her in a boarding school. Marie wouldn't leave France without her daughter and Simon wouldn't leave without his wife, so they stayed.

When the Nazis invaded Paris, Marie, Edmond and little Suzanne fled to Perpignan near the Spanish border to stay with cousins. The Germans weren't there yet. While the family was away, Simon stayed behind in Paris to fight. Marie's father, Avram Wasserman, who went by Adolphe, stayed behind as well. At seventy he felt he was too old to run. But he was not too old to be taken. On September 25, 1942, Marie's father was sent to Auschwitz -- one of seven hundred and twenty Romanian Jews rounded up and never heard from again. Simon, meanwhile, was shot in the leg, captured and held as a prisoner of war. The Red Cross helped secure his release and Simon and the family were reunited in Perpignan.

There, the story goes, Simon bumped into a German guard he befriended when he was a prisoner of war, and now warned to flee. The family escaped to Flayat, where Estelle had been sent for school.

I wondered why Marie hadn't fled there in the first place. Suzanne does not know. Her memories of their time on the run -- and much of her young life -- are fragments she's pieced together from stories she's heard over the years. She tells me that the experience of looking back for her feels as if she is watching a movie where she's the star but doesn't remember being on set. Was it real, or imagined? When the Germans finally leave Paris the entire family returns home. But the joy of homecoming is short lived.

Marie, who had taken Suzanne to the photo studio that day in 1944, died from cancer. She was thirty six. Did she know she was sick and hide it? Had she seen a doctor? For Suzanne, her mother's death is part of the fog of her childhood.

She told me that she once asked her brother, "Did mama love me?"

He replied, "You were a baby."

*

Suzanne remembers sirens blaring, hiding in the subways and the priest who hid them in Flayat. But it's the silence that followed that echoes loudest. Her mother is dead but there's no time to mourn. Nor is there time for her father to fill the void. He has to work. Estelle is eighteen and married and working as well. So Suzanne, who is six, and Edmond who is thirteen, are sent away. Everyone in her family has a role to play. Hers is to go along with things, whether she likes it or not. Even now, she says, "everyone needs to suck it up. I suck it up all the time."

Suzanne doesn't remember the day she was sent to the first orphanage or if her father talked with her and Edmond about where he was taking them. She would live in three different orphanages in three years. She doesn't know if she took a tour first or if she was allowed to bring anything along. Though she thinks she may have had, as she says, a "blankie" because anytime she's had surgery since then, she holds onto a tissue for comfort. She would also keep bread in her pocket. Not because she was hungry but because it felt nice to nibble during the day. Edmond was with her at the first two orphanages. The second one she remembers best. It had about 20 other children and was run by a husband and wife who were Russian Jews. It was said to have been the home of Louis XIV's dentist. Each room, she says, had three "nice" beds. She thinks she was the youngest one there. She remembers a boy named Simon and his two sisters. It felt, she says, like a family.

She doesn't know why she had to move to third. But by then Edmond was fifteen and old enough to work. She hated being left behind. She remembers there were twelve little beds all in a row, like the Madeleine books, but not as sweet. She remembers hurting herself on the metal frame. Her father used to visit on Sundays during all three years. What was said or what they did is like everything else in her past, a mystery. What is known, is that while Suzanne was in the orphanage, Simon was waiting for permission from the United States government to move her and Edmond to Massachusetts, where his relatives lived. Finally, when she was almost nine, the three were approved for passage. The only thing Suzanne had heard about America was that the houses were made out of wood unlike the stone buildings in France. She thought she was being sent to live in a hut. That March, they travelled on an old Navy ship, the DeGrasse. It took eight days to cross the Atlantic. She threw up for seven. When they sailed into New York Harbor she remembers everyone running to see the Statue of Liberty. She remembers it was a nice sunny day.

Her great Aunt Betty and Uncle Solomon picked them up in their car – she remembers they drove a Hudson – and drove them to the home of their cousins Rose and Izzy's house in Rosedale, Queens. After being alone in the orphanage she was now surrounded by family – a family she'd never met and that didn't speak her language. Her father prepared her to say "hi" in English but hi was a hard word for her to pronounce because the French don't pronounce "H's." All that came out as "I." After resting for the night at Rose and Izzy's, her aunt and uncle drove to Worcester, her new home.

There were the wooden houses she'd heard about but instead of huts they were triple-deckers, a common style in town. Her aunt and uncle owned a triple on a small dead end street with lots of kids. One of their tenants had a daughter named Sylvia who became Suzanne's first and dearest friend. Up until that point, Suzanne's relationships with people she loved were fleeting. But her friendship with Sylvia would last sixty years, until Sylvia's death.

She also made friends with the girls down the block, the Cohen sisters, who all fought for the attention of their fifth "sister" Suzanne – as they do to this day. But there was no room for Simon and Edmond to stay at her aunt's house. So once again, she was left behind. She was sixteen when her father died, and now an orphan in every sense of the word. I've never heard her say a harsh word about him.

Decades later, after Jack, who was then in his fifties, had lost both his parents she remembers him sitting, deep in thought. She asked him what was wrong and he shared his sadness over becoming an orphan. She was livid. He was a grown man; imagine what it was like for *her*. Suzanne may have adapted, but she's never gotten over losing her parents when she was so young. Stephen, her middle child, refers to her upbringing as her "trump card." Whenever anyone complains about how bad they had it growing up, Suzanne trumps them with her story. It's hard to compete with Nazis, orphanages and your mother dying when you're four years old. It's become both her burden and badge of honor. That is, until Mari died.

Mari, was her first child and only daughter. Suzanne named her Mari so it would sound the way her mother's name was pronounced in French. Mari was diagnosed with cancer at thirty-six, the same age Marie was when she died. Even though Suzanne was close with all three of her children the bond between the two of them was something different. They fought the way that mothers and daughters do, yet talked on the phone every day. When Mari died, her own daughters were thirteen and nine. After Mari died, busyness was no longer a means of distracting herself from the past but the only way she could keep living in the present. Now, she busied herself in the lives of Alli and Rebecca. In the years since, Suzanne has driven back and forth from New City to Commack countless times, taking them to appointments, showing up for celebrations and taking their calls everyday, sometimes several times a day.

*

I talk with Suzanne and with my own mother too, but because she's my mother and I have loved her all my life, things are more complicated. With Suzanne it is different.

40

We talk about everything and nothing at all. Sometimes it's family gossip other times it's a heart-to-heart. Sometimes I call her to vent about raising a teenager, marveling at how she survived raising three.

She tells me I'm just like her, too hard on myself, that I am an excellent mother. Ten years ago when David and I were having trouble, mostly because I was having my own, she didn't make me feel bad about it or hold it against me for hurting her son. Instead, she told me she loved me and offered unwavering support. A few years later when I finally got sober, she was the third person I told, right after David and my best friend.

She couldn't have been kinder. She told me she wouldn't tell anyone until I was ready, even Jack, and she's kept her word. Suzanne gets an invitation to a Bar Mitzvah and shows up. She attends every funeral, every Christening, every wedding even if she doesn't really know the couple. She is the person who always shows up.

There is a wall in the basement living room of her home dedicated to the past – with photographs of Marie and Simon, and Jack's parents, too. Upstairs there is a memory quilt for Mari, made from pieces of her clothes and covered with photographs. The photograph of her, taken on the long, long ago day her mother took her to the photo studio is elsewhere, and unless you look for it, it is hard to find.

5.

A Country Born Within
Zein Jardaneh

I never planned on betraying my grandmother. It definitely wasn't deliberate, I think. Then again, most betrayal, I'd like to believe, is not a product of extensive foreplaning. If it were, I probably would have chosen a better day, or time, to do it. Not that there's ever a good time to betray a woman who's showered me with unconditional love for the past twenty eight years. If I had planned it better, or at all, I'm sure it wouldn't have happened on the last day I'd have with her for six months, or in front of so many witnesses.

I was leaving for New York that night. The day began like most Fridays in Amman, with my parents, brothers, and I accompanying my grandmother, Intisar, for coffee at her sister-in-law's, a tradition my grandfather began over fifteen years ago, and one we continued after he passed.

My great aunt's living room was crowded that late December morning, with much of the extended family in town for the holidays. Most of us were crammed onto the large U-shaped couch that anchors the room. Conversations varied by which corner of the couch we occupied, until they haphazardly merged into one: Trump's decision to move the American Embassy from Tel Aviv to Jerusalem.

A unified topic did not a unified conversation make. We all talked over each other, loudly, until conversations splintered into couch zones again for manageability. My grandmother sat on the outer edge of one section of the couch, and I sat on the parallel corner, five people and two conversations away. I could see her from the corner of my eye, and could hear her talking, but it was too loud to distill what she was saying. She, on the other hand, managed to hear me say to my uncle that when it came to the Arab-Israeli conflict, we could no longer just look to the past, and our approach needed to be reexamined, given the increasing difficulty of the reality on the ground.

Her shock, and hurt, were palpable. I felt her jump back in her seat, despite our distance and her petite frame. What followed, even amidst the chaotic conversations, was a deafening silence. My grandmother -- a former Jordanian senator, life-long activist, educator and one-time radio host -- was at a loss for words.

She carried her silence all the way to the car, interrupting it briefly only to say goodbye as we left my great aunt's house. I sat in the back seat, waiting, as my father drove with my grandmother in the front passenger seat. Waiting for what, I'm not sure. My grandmother is diplomatic to a fault, and will rarely, if ever, admonish one of her grandchildren out loud. My father could not be of any help in breaking the tension, either. I wasn't sure if he had heard what I had said. Even if he did, he's not one for small talk, or conversations on what could and should have been.

But then, it arrived. That sigh I know all too well. It starts and ends as a whisper. At some point it morphs into a whimper that stems from insurmountable pain. It's a sigh reserved for only the most agonizing of memories: those of my late grandfather, and Palestine.

"You know," she said, speaking to my father, but directing her message to the back seat. "I don't think I could have ever imagined that a day would come where we could differ on Palestine."

I can't remember what happened next. She may have continued talking to my father. My father could have turned on the radio. Or maybe we all just sat in silence. All I know is that the "we" she overtly referred to are the Arabs and the Palestinians. But I was too busy thinking about the veiled "we." The one directed at me, the granddaughter who had accompanied her to countless fundraising dinners, lectures, and events about Palestine. The one who knew that the Palestinian issue was open for discussion, but never for debate. The one who knew that a Palestinian, despite not being born in their country, has their country born within them. The one, who in spite all of this, arrived at a conclusion that morning that elicited that painful sigh.

*

Palestine informs and permeates every aspect of my grandmother's being. It was for Palestine that she first protested at the American University of Beirut. It was there, through Palestine, that she met my grandfather. It was because of Palestine that she became the woman at the forefront of that protest in 1968. Palestine was, and is, the bigger picture. It must be reclaimed. Justice needs to be served. The right of return will be secured. And my grandmother would live trying.

Palestine is also present in the smaller things. It informed how she raised her children -- and how she hoped to influence their children after them. Given the opportunity, she will purchase anything -- from baked goods to furniture -- made by Palestinians, especially if it can help alleviate the suffering of the 2.1 million registered refugees in Jordan. Palestine informed what she does *not* purchase -- if a designer came out in support of Israel, there is no way she'd step foot in their store. If a local grocer in Amman carries produce from Israel, or worse, illegal settlements in the West Bank, not only will she chastise the owner, but she will make damn well sure that everyone boycotts the store as well. Most Muslims pray towards Mecca. She prays towards her hometown of Jerusalem.

The story of how she left Jerusalem has been playing, on loop, in the back of my grandmother's mind, for seventy years. For seventy years, she has thought through every detail, and every step. So much so that she's perfected the narrative, and no gaps remain.

It would also take seventy years before any of her eleven grandchildren would ask her to tell that story from beginning to end. We all knew the basics -- that she was born in Jerusalem in 1936, exiled in 1948, and that she would dedicate her life to her country. For she was one of the last in the family to be born in the country, and not have the country born within.

*

47

My grandmother's unfaltering dedication to Palestine stems from an intimate relationship with loss, disappointment and failure since she became a refugee in 1948.

Her family, she claims, can trace its presence in the city back to the 1500s. Despite rampant political tension between Arabs, the British and Jews during her childhood, the first time she understood the magnitude of what the future could hold came when she was ten. Walking with friends one summer afternoon in July, a large explosion followed by a plume of smoke grabbed their attention. They would soon learn that just a hill over, the Zionist paramilitary group Irgun had carried out its infamous and deadly attack on the King David Hotel, a defining moment in the lead-up to the establishment of Israel.

Things came to a head when in April 1948, Zionist paramilitary groups carried out a massacre in the nearby village of Deir Yassin. Believing the exaggerated death toll claimed by its perpetrators, many Arabs, like my great grandfather, evacuated for what they hoped would be safer grounds, fearing a similar fate.

In May 1948, my great grandfather's intuition was to take his family from their west Jerusalem home to the Old City in the east, believing the move would guarantee their safety. My great aunt and uncle, both married with families at the time, took refuge in the family's property in the Old City. My great grandparents, my grandmother and her youngest brother stayed with family. Packing only a few belongings, thinking that was all they'd need, my grandmother's journey east began. Little did she, or anyone else know, that they'd never return west.

Three of my grandmother's older brothers stayed behind in the family home, purchasing tommy guns and ammunition in case fighting broke out in the neighborhood. One of her brothers, studying in the United States at the time, was spared the experience. My great grandfather had just sold the family's Jericho summer home; cash would be more valuable than assets if the crisis continued to escalate. Wanting to maintain access to the money, he placed it in a tin candy box, leaving the box under his sons' care.

Within days of arriving to the Old City, the family received news that their neighborhood was under attack, and that Zionist paramilitary groups had taken over much of the area. My grandmother feared the worst: her brothers who remained behind had surely been killed or captured. Her relatives shielded her father from the painful trip, scoping out the situation in his stead, only to find my great uncles fleeing. Out of ammunition (and Arab soldiers stationed nearby had none to spare) my great uncles decided that their only option was to join the family in the Old City. In their rush to safety, they left the tin box behind.

My great grandfather still held hope that they would return home once fighting subsided. Their living situation in East Jerusalem, even in the short term, was unsustainable. A wealthy merchant, he leveraged his connections and secured temporary housing for his family in Halhoul, a village near Hebron. My grandmother, like many others at the time, remained in denial. Her memories of the period in Halhoul are fond ones, filled with days spent in the garden with children her age.

While in Halhoul, my great grandfather eventually realized that any chances of going back home had all but dissipated, and any next steps needed to align with that reality. He was able to reach friends in Amman who set the family up in a home that would adequately serve their needs. My great grandfather relocated to Amman permanently, never to live in Palestine, or the same country as most of his children, again.

Two of his seven children, Hussnieh and Taleb, lived the remainder of their lives in East Jerusalem. Mohammad, pursuing his Ph.D. at Wisconsin-Madison in 1948, briefly returned to the Middle East, ultimately settling in Rome before succumbing to cancer in 1997. Rajab moved with the family to Amman, but given the circumstances, could not continue his university education in order to help his father reestablish himself in Jordan. Badawi's life was claimed by a stray bullet that pierced a wall in his home in Amman during Black September, a period of brief civil war between the Palestinian Liberation Organization and the Jordanian government in 1970. A government-imposed curfew prevented his immediate burial in the family cemetery outside of Amman, forcing the family to bury him temporarily in Rajab's backyard. My grandmother and her younger brother, Kamal, were fortunate enough to have been enrolled in schools in East Jerusalem, the part of the city that remained under Arab control after the *Nakba* -- the "catastrophe" of the end of Palestine that came with the birth of Israel. They were sent to live with Hussnieh and Taleb to continue their education and maintain some sense of normalcy. My grandmother left Jerusalem in 1954 for the American University of Beirut. Kamal left Jerusalem for Germany in 1956, where he would go on to earn a medical degree and continue to reside in until this day.

While my grandmother frequently visited her siblings in East Jerusalem, it wasn't until 1972, five years after Israel occupied the West Bank, that she was able to go back to her old neighborhood in West Jerusalem.

In town for her brother-in-law's funeral, distant relatives managed to get permission to take her to West Jerusalem. Driving up to the house, she saw a large "beware of the dog" sign on the front gate. Upon arriving at the house, she recalls, she was so overcome with emotion that all she could do was sob hysterically, and could not step out of the car. Later, she would learn, that the three-story house was divided into several apartments, and that the Israeli government had taken ownership of what had been their home.

Driving back from her old neighborhood to her sister's house in East Jerusalem, my grandmother couldn't help but notice that despite the occupation, nothing had changed. She could still identify friend's homes, every corner, and every street. "It was so well built, it was so beautiful," she says. "I'm sure they knew they didn't need to change much."

*

I don't know exactly when I became aware of the fact that I am Palestinian. I was born and raised in Amman, as was my father, and his father before him. My mother, on the other hand, was born in Jerusalem.

I do, however, remember how I became aware of Israel, and its proximity to Jordan. I couldn't have been more than five. It had to be sometime between Oslo I and Oslo II. Probably around the time that Jordan was negotiating its peace treaty with Israel. The Arab-Israeli conflict was surely being discussed more than usual in order for my younger self to realize that this was something that I should be aware of. Something I should fear.

A friend and I were sprawled out on the floor of our family room, thumbing through an atlas. I vividly remember getting to a section with an enlarged map of the Middle East and recognizing Jordan. Much to my surprise, there it was, right next us: Israel. I remember my shock and looking up to find my mother, seeking her for comfort. The map must be wrong. When my mother finally arrived, she laughed, presumably at my innocence, and told me she could do very little to change Jordan's location on the map, or Israel's.

And it was along these lines that my Palestinian identity began to take shape. It was molded by fear -- fear of what had been lost, and what we stood to lose. It was engrained in school, when every morning at lineup, we would sing the Jordanian national anthem along with *Mawtini* — my country -- the official anthem of the Palestinian cause, but to the dismay of many, not the state. In high school, I was a regular participant of the Jerusalem Committee, an annual interscholastic competition between Jordanian high schools where students would present a research paper about the issue du jour as it pertained to Palestine. And every year, come presentation day, some judge or the other would ask if and how I was related to Intisar Jardaneh. I would confirm that I am, indeed, her granddaughter. The response almost always was, "but of course."

Then there was life. My first and only visit to Palestine and Israel was in the summer of 1998. We crossed into Palestine through the King Hussein Bridge by car, where my mother was singled out for additional interrogation -- her Canadian passport and birthplace raising red flags for the Israeli officers operating the borders. Two years later the second *Intifada* -- uprising -- began. On the *Intifada's* second day, Muhammad Al Durrah and his father would get caught in the crossfire between Israeli and Palestinian armed forces. Despite his father's best attempts at shielding Muhammad and pleading for safety, an Israeli bullet would claim the twelve-year-old's life. He was just a year older than I was.

Going to college at seventeen, I believed it my duty to change perceptions about Palestinians. To make sure that people would take our side. The right side. We are, after all, the victims of Jewish and foreign aggression, and it is our God-given right to play that card, and fight for a cause we unquestionably believe in. I wore my Palestinian-ness like a badge of honor: my people were wronged, I was lucky to be a Palestinian and I was going to let everyone and their mother know it. Armed with the environment of political activism I grew up in, and the emphasis placed at home about knowing the ins-and-outs of the conflict, I was prepared to fight.

But again, life would rear its confounding head. I gradually, and painfully, began to realize that while I could not, and did not want to, recognize Israel's right to exist, it existed. I spent most of my formative years struggling with denial and anger. In college, I bargained. Now, my depression evolved into acceptance.

Leaving my Palestinian echo chamber shook me to my core. Everything I held to be true was now in question. Zionism and Judaism are not the same. Some American Jews are more sympathetic to the Palestinian cause than most. American Christians can be more Zionist than Israelis. Another shocking revelation: those big bad Israelis? Many are nice, too.

Then came the unthinkable: I began resenting my Palestinian-ness. I resented that there seemed to be only one right way to be one. I resented that I had to fight tooth and nail to be the right kind of Palestinian, while those who should have worked tirelessly to protect my Palestinian-ness continued to fail me. I resented that along with that identity came the burden of seventy years of gray in a conflict that I had only learned about in black and white. I resented that my rational self understood that the parameters of discussion had to change drastically, but my emotional self is laden with guilt when I'm too pragmatic.

Most of all, I resent that despite a long, cerebral conversation with a classmate about the conflict, I lost all sense of decorum upon her stating that the "separation wall" kept "terrorists" out of Israel, resulting in various outbursts about how the terrorists she referred to are many of my relatives still living in the West Bank. I resent that I need to be twice as informed when talking about the open-air prison that is the Gaza Strip, the razing of Palestinian homes, and Arab-Israelis being treated as third-class citizens. I resent the permanently etched memories of each my grandmothers' faces when they, repeatedly, could not cross into the West Bank for family members' funerals. I resent that when my mother inherited land in Halhoul upon my grandfather's passing, my family and I had to discuss whether to keep the land in order to maintain a connection to him, and to Palestine, at the risk of it being usurped by settlers and becoming an illegal settlement.

*

We often speak of the *Nakba* as something that began and ended in 1948. So much so that when Israel would occupy the West Bank in 1967, we would give the outcome of the Six Day War a new name, *Naksa* -- the setback. But for my grandmother, even though life's fortunes would be kinder to her than many of the millions who share her fate, the *Nakba* never ended. She lives, and relives, those last days in Jerusalem, the life away from Jerusalem, every day. She wakes up to a *Nakba* and sleeps to a *Naksa*.

I don't think the *Nakba* ever ended for me, either. Not sharing the nostalgia for what was makes my *Nakba* different from my grandmother's. It makes it easier for me, at some levels, to forgive. Often, it also makes me forget. Forget that it exists and forget what it has done.

I have not spoken with my grandmother about that Friday in Amman. And I've wrestled with why. There certainly have been plenty of opportunities to do so -- we've talked, at length, about Palestine, as it was, and as it is, since.

Maybe it's because after years of my father drilling the concept of the futility of conversations on what could and should have been, I've finally learnt that there are some things that are better left unsaid. I know that if I were to broach the subject again, my grandmother will engage me with an open mind. Her heart, deeply scarred seventy years on, may not be as receptive.

Maybe it's because I've resigned myself to the fact that while she's a spritely eighty-two-year-young woman, every moment and conversation I have with her is precious, and I'll never know when it'll be the last.

Maybe it's because deep down, despite what unfolded that Friday morning, I know she knows we are two sides of the same coin. That she knows that while I have reshaped the mantle she so fervently passed on, its purpose remains the same. And that she knows that the generation who experienced the *Nakba* may be dwindling, but the young will never relinquish their dreams, and will never forget.

6.

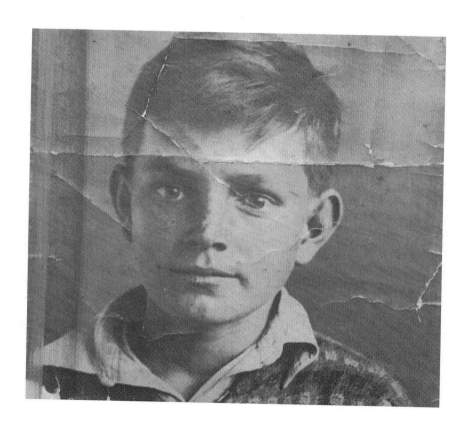

Moonshine
Will McCollister

"Faye," my Aunt Kathy called out to my mother as we were sifting through the boxes of photos in my recently deceased grandmother's spare bedroom. "Come look at this."

The faint smell of stale cinnamon candy that she kept on the dresser still lingered. My grandmother had died earlier that December, and now her daughters were culling through old photographs that no one else might ever see. My Aunt Kathy was cleaning out a separate room when she called for my mom. I can still remember walking into the room -- I was fifteen-years- old - and hearing my mother say, "I need this."

She held out an old, wrinkled photo that looked to have been buried beneath the others for years. It was of a boy. He was maybe nine-years-old with messy hair, freckles, worn clothing, and a piercing stare. It was the eyes -- the eyes looked straight through me as if to say, "What the hell are you looking at?"

"Do you know who this is?" my mother asked I shrugged my shoulders and asked, "Who?"

"This," she said, "is your grandfather, James."

I had never seen a picture of my grandfather, let alone one of him as a child. He was as much a stranger to you as he is to me, his grandson. He died in 1977 at the age of fifty two, long before I was born. The little that I knew about him came at family gatherings when my uncles would swap stories or say things to me like, "Well there's no doubt you're James Hall's grandson."

Even then I noticed something was wrong. Why was it that every time we talked about my grandfather the conversation was always cut short? One day after church, my mother and I were walking back to the car and as she opened the door I asked her, "Mom, did you love pawpaw?"

*

To understand my grandfather you have to understand eastern Kentucky, not it is today, but as was in 1925, the year he was born. The coalfields of Pike and Boyd counties were the breeding grounds of poverty and the failed American state. Some men were lucky enough to make it to the age of forty, but the others gave their lives to the mines. My great-grandfather, Tige, was a farmer and a coal miner. He needed people to work on the farm, so he married my great-grandmother Arminda and they began having children. James was the fifteenth and last of those children, three of which died before he was born. One died of pneumonia as a small child, a common occurrence back then, and two of his older brothers met violent ends. My grandfather was born into a world of chaos.

The farm was enough to keep the family from starving, but this was not the life any of them wanted. My great-grandfather, Tige had grown up the son of a banker and had inherited the farm, but like many people in Eastern Kentucky he had fallen on hard times. Prohibition was then in its fourth year, and the answer to their problems was moonshine.

Whoever it was that started running the shine from the family farm is unclear, but one thing is certain, Bill and Lee, my grandfather's older brothers were involved. After a long shift in the coalmine people needed a drink, so bootleggers, like my great uncles, obliged. Family lore aside, there was nothing romantic or complicated about this: they were drug dealers. And with that came dire consequences. Bill was shot in a duel in front of his family. Lee was poisoned. The deaths of his two oldest sons drove Tige to alcoholism.

By the time the Great Depression began to ravage eastern Kentucky, Tige could only find comfort in the bottom of a whiskey glass, and it tore his family apart. Arminda left him, leaving my grandfather without a home. She found a place of her own but there was no room for him.

He dropped out of school by third grade. He moved from house to house, shipped off to whichever older sibling could accommodate him. Tige could no longer care for him, and Arminda, who had once provided the only stability in his life, was dying of stomach cancer. Her death, I was told, devastated him. He was eight years old, effectively an orphan. He began to smoke and drink.

He was sixteen when he tried to enlist. The army caught him, so he tried his luck with the Navy. He served on a destroyer escort in the Pacific until his appendix burst and he was sent home, to eastern Kentucky. He married my grandmother, Ruby, who had grown up a sharecropper's daughter so poor that until she married had never slept on a real bed and who had also dropped out of school in third grade. They would have nine children, and in time leave Kentucky, but only go as far as Coal Grove, a small village across the Ohio River from where he grew up. My mother was the oldest girl. But it would fall to her brothers to introduce me to the legend of my grandfather.

*

At family gatherings it was like clockwork. My Uncle Larry, a burly steelworker and the oldest of my grandfather's sons, would grab me by the shoulders, and ask, "Boy, when are you going come hunting with me?" in his boisterous Appalachian twang. Then the stories would begin. He would start with adventure tales about frontiersmen like Simon Kenton or Daniel Boone who, he said with pride, lived not far where our family was from. From there he would turn to stories about his uncle Bill, the bootlegger, and made a point of showing me how big he was. By this point my cousins would have gathered around and Larry would grow animated, as the stories got bolder and wilder. We were rapt, and shocked, even though these were stories he had told us many times before.

There was the story about how Bill came home late one night and woke my great-grandfather Tige. Bill's brother-in-law had turned on him, and was coming to kill him. He needed his father's advice. Bill had caught wind that his brother-in-law would be wearing armor that acted like a bulletproof vest, and he needed to know how to kill him.

"Shoot him in the neck," said Tige. That Sunday Bill waited in the church, calmly rubbing his fingers against the grip of a pistol he had placed in the pocket of his trousers, knowing the minute he stepped outside all hell would break loose. The service ended. Bill walked out the front door to see his brother-in-law waiting for him. The two stared each other down. Bill drew his pistol and fired, hitting his brother-in-law in the throat, but not before he was shot in the chest. Bill was wounded badly, but was talking to Tige on the way to the hospital. Even a bullet couldn't kill Bill Hall.

"And pawpaw Tige swears the doctors let Bill die," Uncle Larry would say pointing at each of us huddled around him.

The stories were thrilling, Bunyan-esque, and they didn't stop there. Because then came the tales of my grandfather. James Hall, he began, was a legendary brawler. If you ran into him at a bar, you'd better have two guns and a couple other guys with you.

He lived by one rule, Uncle Larry told us: "You never start a fight, but you damn sure better never run away from one."

He was six-foot-four, broad shouldered and could outpunch anyone that dared challenge him, even the Marines he took on one night in a bar in California – maybe five of them, Uncle Larry said, or maybe a dozen.

"He was holdin' his own against 'em," my uncle would tell us. "He backed up into a corner so each of 'em would come at him one at a time," Larry would mimic each blow with his fists swishing through the air. "One of 'em decided to break a beer bottle and throw it at him. It caught him right across the eye," said my uncle, slowly gestured across the bottom of his eyelid.

Somehow my grandfather got out of the place and got to the doctor, his eye barely hanging on by a thread. The doctor took out a glass and poured it full of alcohol, and brushed the sand off of my grandfather's eye.

"The doctor took his eye and dipped it in the glass and

popped it right back in!" my uncle would say.

We all wanted to be like Bill. We all wanted to be like James.

My mother never interrupted. I have no clear memories of her being in the room, or trying to stop him. My father, who had heard the stories too, would repeat them from time to time. But neither he nor my mother could compete with Uncle Larry. Still, there was another James Hall I was vaguely aware of, the one who my mother had endured as a father, the one I heard almost nothing about.

*

My cousin got married in Chicago last year and there was an open bar. People drink at weddings and though I not much of a drinker – my escape was school and especially sports -- I wanted to celebrate. I had two beers. I was sober, yet I could feel my mother staring a hole through me as I took each sip. We returned home to southern Ohio the next day and were greeted by my sister, who asked us about the wedding.

"It was beautiful," said my mother. "It was great, but Will really enjoyed the open bar."

I grew up in a home where there was no alcohol, not even a glass of wine at dinner. That was not the case in the house where my mother grew up.

When my mom was a child there were nights when my grandfather would not come home, nights when he would just stay at the bar until it was time to go to work the next morning. The nights that he would come home were the nights that my mother prayed. She prayed that the happy drunk would come home and tell his adventure stories about his big brother Bill – not the angry drunk whose behavior she chooses not to elaborate on beyond saying it was "abusive." He had by then left the mines and became an ironworker and while the money was good, he spent it on liquor. They lived in a farmhouse that looked like something from 1860 rather than 1960. No heat, no electricity, no running water.

Life in her home was reduced a guessing game of which

James Hall was going to show up. Alcohol had ruined his own father's marriage and life. My grandfather had spent virtually all his life drinking, stopping only a few years before he died.

My Uncle Larry used to tell me there was no denying I was James Hall's grandson. I look like my mother and she looks so much like her father that now, as she looks in the mirror, she can see the growing resemblance, especially around the eyes.

I have never given my parents reason to worry, and yet the mere sight of me having a Miller Lite and then a second was enough to disappoint my mother deeply.

I look at the picture of my grandfather as a boy and the words that come to mind are "damaged" and "broken." He is nine-years-old. He never escapes.

I was his age the day at my grandmother's house when she began to talk about my grandfather. I don't want to talk about that now, said my mother. She never wanted to talk about him. The question I asked her that day – "did you love pawpaw?" – seemed so innocent.

Her answer still rings in my ears.

"I don't know."

7.

Perfection's Infection
Reh Blazier

I've come to look at perfection as an infection, a hereditary condition that's found its way from my mother's genes to mine. I am not perfect, and neither is my mother. But that hasn't stopped either of us from striving for, and failing to attain, perfection.

This need for perfection didn't start with my mother, and I doubt it will end with her. Two birds of a feather go down dark paths together, or something like that.

No, perfection's infection did not start with my mother or even her mother. It must have started with her father, the ghost I hold responsible for our continued affliction.

*

His name was Frank Reh and a lifetime ago, he was my mother's father. I never met Frank. He exists in stories and photographs, mentioned by my mother in passing with venom in her voice. He lives as a caricature in my mind with gold-rimmed glasses, lips pursed beneath a mustache, standing with hands clasped below his stomach in the brown tuxedo he wore to my mother's wedding.

My mother and older brother inherited Frank's lithe frame, their bodies stretching high above my own, limbs taut and defined compared to what I call my "Midwest body." Our noses resemble his, or so I am told. Straight bridges hooked at the downward slope near nostrils that flare when we're angry, perplexed, or in the case of my older brother, when he is judging a person from afar.

*

I can't bring myself to call Frank "grandpa" or "großvater," whatever he might have prefered. Especially not in a way that evokes familial fondness. How is it possible to love someone you've never met? I do not know the sound of his voice and whether its intonations betrayed his Germanic roots. I never wondered what it might have felt like to hug him on Christmas morning, his coffee spilling as my toddler body slammed into his.

I have not seen his handwriting in a card wishing me well or scribbled on a birthday check year after year. I do not know his smile, whether it was toothless and rotting like my grandmother's the last time I saw her.

But knowing what I know, it would not have mattered if I called him Frank, some kind of father or what he really was. A fucker. I know which I prefer.

*

Here is what I know. Frank Reh was the son of first generation German immigrants. He was born sometime in November at some hospital in some town that only matters to those who live and die there. Frank died there.

Frank worked as a dairy farmer, just like his father and his father before him. Equipped with a high school education and not much else, Frank married Vivian June Gilbertson at the St. Charles Borromeo Catholic Church in the winter of 1952. Almost nine months later, the first of five Reh daughters, Deborah, entered the world.

*

My mother was not the first Reh daughter and she was not the last. She's the child in the middle, just like me.

Ask a middle child, any middle child, and they'll tell you about all the attention they didn't receive. I say it jokingly. My mother says it seriously. As one of five daughters, my mother did not stand out. Her mother loved animals. Her father loved no one.

*

I am my mother's only daughter and prefer it that way. Sandwiched between two brothers, I share a bond with my mother they cannot replicate. When I was younger, I could not see the physical resemblance between us. But as I grow into my body, it's become easier to see her square jaw in the mirror, her hooded eyes, and the shape of her asymmetrical smile reciprocating mine.

I am my mother's only daughter and perhaps it's best that way. We need each other in ways we need no one else, and for that, I am thankful.

*

A photograph sits to the right hand of my mother on her nightstand. The nightstand, an antique desk circa the early 1900s, was repurposed to store tubes of lotion, mesh racks laced with hooped earrings, weather-worn books and half-filled dream journals.

The photo, taken on an August weekend in Northern Arizona, lives in a modern silver frame, juxtaposing the man and woman in focus. I know enough about the photo and Arizona summers to tell you it was likely twenty degrees over one hundred in The Valley of the Sun, and driving two hours north meant respite to cooler, welcome weather.

The man's face in the photo is tanned but partially obscured. I know from a lifetime of looking at him that the lower half of my father's face was shrouded beneath a black beard I've never seen him without. Thirty years later, the beard holds more silver and grey, but my dad is still tan, perhaps permanently so.

The smile on the woman's face, my mother's face, stands out more than her pregnant belly. Her mouth is not open enough to show a full-toothy grin. She's smizing -- smiling with her eyes -- a term Tyra Banks does not get enough credit for coining.

My mother is grasping my father's wrists, pulling his face toward hers. This is Larry and Carol, forever suspended in a moment of bliss, seconds before a goodbye kiss, only three months until the birth of their first child.

Neither of my parents knew the baby in my mother's belly, nor did they know I'd come along three years later. They didn't know their youngest son would be born with Down syndrome or that they'd celebrate their fortieth wedding anniversary in 2018. They certainly didn't know they'd own an acre lot in Phoenix, complete with three dogs, two horses, one goat, the neighbor's chickens and a cat that would outlive every animal just mentioned. The house would be filled with teenagers, too much dog hair and birthday parties people still text me about today.

It was impossible to predict their future, and just as impossible to erase their pasts.

Larry and Carol may not have known what their lives held beyond the moment captured in the photograph, yet they knew what happened six months prior.

You see, in the photo in the silver frame placed on the right-hand-side of my mother's nightstand-desk, someone captured romance in the last weeks of a 1989 Arizona summer, when it did not matter to my mother that my grandfather killed himself in March. This was just my mom and dad, happy to love one another, and grateful to forget Frank, if only for a moment.

*

I wish I could remember when I first found out about Frank's suicide, but when I ask my dad if he remembers finding out, I rethink the macabre desire.

It was March, March 15, 1989 to be exact. My father returned home from work to see the red light on the voicemail blinking. Kathy, my mother's sister, left a message. How does one leave a message saying their father is dead and not by natural causes? My dad can't recall the exact verbiage used and it doesn't matter. The facts remain the same.

Vivian left for work, and before doing so, turned to Frank, whose untreated depression left him voluntarily incapacitated on the couch, picking lint so vigorously, holes bore into the fabric.

"Don't do anything stupid," she told him. She must have known. In the days before Frank walked into the garage, closed the car door, cracked the windows and turned the ignition, he threatened to kill my grandmother and aunt Gwen.

"If we were all dead, all of our problems would be gone," Frank told his wife and daughter.

"Well, all your problems would be," Gwen replied. "But I want to live."

My mom thinks Gwen's response saved her and Vivian. Frank owned a shotgun, and my mom said she thought he had it in him to kill.

What was it like growing up with a father like that? The story makes me think of my own father who has never owned a gun. I have been on the receiving end of his angriest looks, but could never, would never, say my own father was capable of killing my mother and me.

My mother maintains she was not surprised to learn of her father's death. She always knew he would end things himself. Perhaps that's why, when she made her way back to Illinois for Frank's funeral, my mother leaned over the casket and looked at Frank for the final time.

"That was really stupid," she whispered to his corpse. "That was really stupid."

*

Stories of my mother's childhood differ greatly from stories of my own. She grew up on a dairy farm with cattle, horses and wild cats that lived in the barn. In the summer, my mom and her sisters rode the horses down to a creek on the family's property for hours of adventure only allotted to children of her generation.

My mother's happier memories include riding horses and feeding barn cats milk straight from a cow's udder. They do not include the times rats crawled through holes in the shower walls. The humiliation of her mother having to work at the Playskool factory. The time her father called her a bitch.

Her childhood was not one of physical abuse, but scars still linger. She recalls Frank's indifference toward her existence, until it came time to unleash an inventory of insults.

Straight A's in all classes except Physical Education? Why didn't you do better?
Magna Cumme Laude in nursing school? Thank god you didn't end up pregnant. I thought for sure you would have. And by the way, your car is in the shop. Engine's busted.

Nothing my mother did was ever good enough, and if Frank did one thing as a father, it was make sure my mother never forgot that.

*

When I look at the photo of my parents, of course I see the beauty in it. But I also see Frank, or at least think of him. Six months gone, but no longer a part of my parents' lives. My mom wanted to escape her imperfect family, and in this photo, she is looking toward the future of her own family. Her own perfect family.

But our family was not perfect. And there is no real way to trace the trajectory of my family's imperfection. I can point to Frank and say, "This is your fault." But it's not, not really. Well, not all of it.

*

When I think back to the happiest moments of my childhood, they include summers in our swimming pool. My brothers and I watching as my dad pulled his 1985 El Camino into the side yard, stripping off his sweat-soaked work clothes, tossing jeans, a t-shirt, his steel-toed boots into a pile of rocks, and cannonballing into a pool of shrieking children. The days I remember smelled like sunscreen, chlorine and pool water on the blistering concrete.

My least favorite memories aren't from childhood, but late adolescence. July in Arizona, when the heat and proximity to my parents threatened to suffocate me.

I decided to step out of perfection's narrative and into my own. One filled with anxiety, depression, and a toxic relationship. I embraced imperfection and accepted the feelings I could not control if it meant coping. A radical idea, considering my background. But I was abrupt in my decision. I did not prepare my family for such a change. When you spend so long pretending everything is alright, people don't want to accept you're anything but.

I think of the transgressions committed in my admission of - what was it? Mediocrity? Imperfection? Humanity.

Why are you so sad?
Why are you so selfish?
Haven't you been given everything?

*

There's a radical juxtaposition between my mother and me, and it has everything to do with her upbringing. When she wanted to be a doctor, her father told her no.

"You can be a nurse," he told her. "That's good enough."

When I wanted to be a writer, a journalist, move to New York, my mother never told me no. She would never let the violent impact of "no" destroy my dreams. She knew better.

I've never asked my mother if she loved her father. I don't think I need to.

8.

Along Came Shirley

Sage Kendahl Howard

T he hospital called my grandfather when she died, just as he had arranged. He knew she was failing rapidly and so he kept calling to check on her condition. He was to be the one who would call the television stations to let them know she had died but when he did, he had to convince them that the call was not a hoax, that Shirley Chisholm had died and that it had fallen to him to make the calls. But the people at the television stations had never heard of my grandfather even though he had been with her since the beginning. It was painful for him, having to explain himself, having to convince the television people who he had been in her life. He told them to check their archives, because then they would see that he was who he claimed to be.

He called CNN, ABC and NBC, because many years before she had been an important person, the first black woman to serve in Congress and the first woman to run for President. That was in 1972. But now it was New Year's Day, 2005, and Shirley Chisholm had died of a stroke in a Florida hospital, far from her home in Brooklyn, far from my grandfather.

He gave interview after interview, standing by the fireplace in his Brooklyn home. There was a picture on the mantle of him and Shirley that he showed to the reporters. Afterwards my grandmother teased him. "What, you think this is the last time you're going to be on TV?"

"I was the last man standing who was there from the beginning," my grandfather told me. "Everyone else is dead."

I had come to talk with him about Shirley Chisholm and about him, and how it was that he had spent so much of his working life devoted to her. My grandparents have been married for fifty five years and I have never doubted my grandfather's love and devotion to my grandmother. But all the same, Shirley Chisholm had been a part of his life. He talked about her the way that my grandmother would talk about relatives. He worked for her in Congress, and even after she retired and others moved on with their lives, he remained at her side.

But why? What had drawn my grandfather to Shirley Chisholm? Why was he the last man standing?

*

"What is the first thing that comes to mind when someone asks you about Shirley?" I ask my grandfather.

"The first thing that comes to mind," he says, "is I miss her."

I do not remember the first time I heard of Shirley Chisholm. She wasn't a member of my family, but my grandfather spoke about her as if she was. As a little girl, I only thought of her in the context of a black and white family photo that sat on the mantle at my grandparent's house, the same photo my grandfather showed reporters the day Shirley died. She was the woman standing next to my grandfather who wasn't my grandmother. In fact, I heard her name spoken more in my grandparents' home than I did in any history class.

My grandfather, William Howard Sr., was twenty three years old when, in 1967, Shirley Chisholm came into the bank where he worked to congratulate him on becoming the first black secretary of Metropolitan Savings Bank in Bedford-Stuyvesant. "If you were black with that title working in a bank, you had to be light skin," he says, reminding me that his deep-brown skin did not get him the job. There were write-ups about him in several Brooklyn newspapers and Shirley and her aide Wesley Holder came to see him.

"She was just an average person that came to the bank," my grandfather recalled. But before she left she asked him, "Do you have any political interests?"

"No," he replied.

"How about you come down to some of the meetings for

76

our political club," she suggested and left the time and the address for their next event.

He decided he would go, but with no real expectations. That would change the day Shirley told him her true intentions. "The day she indicated to me that she wanted to run for the U.S. congress," he said. "I woke up."

My grandfather could not fathom the guts a black woman had to have to believe she could organize a campaign, and win a seat in Congress. From that moment on he would be at her side. A year later, in 1968, she won her seat.

Shirley Chisholm was born in Brooklyn, but when she was still very young her parents returned to Barbados. The family returned to Brooklyn when Shirley was not yet an adolescent. She graduated from Brooklyn College and then earned a graduate degree from Teachers College at Columbia University. She planned to become a teacher. But she was not destined for the classroom. Shirley, it is fair to say, did not shy from speaking her mind, to anyone. She spoke directly and forcefully and without a hint of being deferential. When she attended meetings for her local community board and political clubs, leaders treated her like a troublemaker. She would go directly to politicians with questions and concerns that no one else was addressing. Though she knew the leaders never had answers, she'd continue to prod just to see their responses. Other women who belonged to these community organizations did not behave this way. It wasn't long before she caught the attention of political organizers like Wesley Holder, the man who became her campaign manager.

In Congress, she was made to feel isolated by her fellow representatives, most of them white and male. When they did not invite her to join them for lunch, she took a seat with them just the same. In 1972 she sought the Democratic presidential nomination, and though her campaign was dismissed as quixotic -- even the men of the Black Congressional Caucus did not support her -- the fact that she believed herself ready to be President spoke volumes about her considerable self-assurance, and self-regard.

By this time, my grandfather had been with her for five years, and his position on her campaigns gave him a first-class ticket on what was known as "Shirley's Chisholm Trail" -- a big deal for a young black man good with numbers who had escaped the brutality of segregated North Carolina during America's great migration.

*

"The last time I actually sat on this side of the living room was when a reporter was interviewing me right after Chisholm's death," he said to me as I pulled my chair closer to him. This side of the living room is usually reserved for special occasions, like taking family photos.

It was ten in the morning and he was still in his pajamas and unshaven.

I asked, "What is your fondest memory of her?"

"I guess traveling with her."

"And what was that like?"

"Well a lot of times when we traveled we had to go to four or five different political events," he said. "And many of those political events you had to get out on a dance floor. So I was always out on the dance floor with Chisholm."

When he said this, I began to think of my grandmother.

My grandmother, Cordelia Howard, was a shy sixteen-year-old Panamanian migrant when she met my grandfather. They met at a friend's birthday party. At first, my she wanted nothing to do with "Billie," and even urged her aunt to send him away when he popped up at their apartment the day after they met. She remembers the day clearly. She had finally managed to put her thick long hair in rollers, and she was in the midst of drying it when he arrived.

"Make him go away," she said to her aunt. Her aunt refused.

He'd take her out dancing, and on trips to Bear Mountain, where she packed rice and peas and potato salad. He found her an apartment to move into when her mother arrived in New York, and when the time was right, he asked her to marry him. My grandfather was the one and only man who courted her after she left the warmth of her home country for a city she has never really loved.

My grandmother says that if she were more outgoing she would have become a singer and traveled the world. Instead she opted for something more low-key -- Brooklyn, and my grandfather, and her three children.

"But what about Shirley?" I asked.

My grandparents had already been married for five years and had two children when she met Shirley. She remembers meeting her at a fund raising event my grandfather hosted in their home. This was the day they took the photo that had caught my eye as a child -- the one that so resembles a family photo and in which my grandfather stood between both women.

"Eh... She was West Indian," my grandmother said, alluding to Shirley's Bajan accent, and her no-play attitude. "She sounded tough, and she looked like she was a boss. She liked telling people what to do, and what not to do."

When my father was born in 1963, my grandmother was not sure whether my grandfather actually wanted a family. "He had other plans," she says. What those plans were became clearer, four years later when Shirley walked into the bank, and into their lives.

"When we would go to any affairs, he paid all the attention to her, and I'm like 'hellooo, I thought I was the wife here?'" she told me. "But after a while I got used to it."

My grandmother had gone from feeling like the center of my grandfather's universe, to the woman who reared his kids during the day, and occasionally accompanied him to events at night. I've often wondered who was actually at fault in this situation: my grandmother for subjecting herself to events she did not want to attend, or my grandfather for making her feel ignored? I am still unsure, in part my grandfather remembers things so differently.

He boasts about how much my grandmother enjoyed the events he'd take her to when he was able to get an extra ticket. He says her favorite part was meeting the people she would watch on television. When I looked around the living room at the photos in which my grandmother appears, she is smiling, and even a little joyful.

*

In 1977, after two terms in congress, and after divorcing her husband of twenty eight years, Shirley remarried and considered not seeking reelection.

"She wanted to be happy," my grandfather said. The prospect of her leaving office upset him. He says he told her she couldn't walk away from power, because she'd never get it back. Out of spite, he told a reporter that Shirley had done nothing for him. The story ran, and when Shirley learned of, it she responded, in her characteristically blunt way.

"'Well maybe I didn't help him with his career, but I nurtured him,'" she told the same reporter.

"So, do you not think she nurtured you at all?" I asked.

"Not only did she nurture me, but she nurtured everyone in this house," he replied.

"Remember, I had three children. When Chisholm would come to this house, the first thing she would do is ask William, Lisa, and Chris 'Let me see your report cards.'"

My father's memories align with both his parents.

"She reminded me of a school teacher," he said.

He was nine years old when his father took him to meet her. She was expecting my grandfather to drive her to an event. When she met his son, she treated him the way she treated everyone else. She immediately put him to work.

"She met me and she said 'Okay, I got something for you to do. Carry this purse,'" he said. "She always did that when she saw me. Made me carry her pocketbook."

He also remembers the fundraising parties his parents hosted, and how as he got older his friends at school asked if he knew her. He'd tell his friends "yeah, she was just at my house just the other night!"

"She was a black woman, and she was right there in the halls of Congress making up laws for this country," he said. "I thought that was incredible. She's the Obama story, before Obama. And a bunch of guys from Bed-Stuy and Crown Heights ran the campaign to get her into Congress."

But then, he added, "The thing with your grandfather is, he wants to give back to the point that it's a fault."

80

I could feel the sharpness of this comment. At first I didn't quite understand how he could feel this way. But as he spoke it all started to make sense.

"I mean all the vacations I went on, were with my mother," he said. "I can't even remember if I went to a movie with my father."

*

My grandfather sits across from me, leaning to one side of his chair. Physically, he takes up much less space than in the photos that surround us. Photos of him and my grandmother with all the politicians he knew are hidden among school photos of graduating grandchildren.

Each of the rooms in their home is cluttered with folders, newspaper clippings, and old speeches. My grandfather saves them for the occasional reporter, or historian. Their home feels like the center of the Shirley Chisholm Legacy Foundation.

"What is the first thing that comes to mind when someone asks you of Shirley?" I ask my grandfather.

"The first thing that comes to mind is I miss her. I miss her because she would be on the forefront of all of the issues that relate to the continuation of the black race," he says in the very rehearsed political-talking-head manner he's answered all my other questions.

Once we are done, my grandfather pulls himself together to retreat to his bedroom, where he showers, and gets dressed. An hour later, my grandmother fusses with him about remembering to take his medication. He kisses her goodbye, and is off to meetings in the same Brooklyn neighborhoods that Shirley Chisholm represented in Congress, when he was a young man, always at her side.

9.

He Didn't Con Her
J. W. Kash

When Tino DeAngelis died, my grandmother called my mother and mentioned his death, and that there wasn't a funeral or a wake for him. My grandmother was always private about her relationship with Tino. But my mother went to her house anyway after the phone call, without telling her she was coming. When my mother arrived, my grandmother cried, saying,

"You came."

Tino was seventy one when he met my grandmother. He was renting her sister's house. My grandfather died a few weeks after he moved in. Tino sent an extravagant bouquet of flowers to my grandfather's wake. Then he began taking my grandmother out to dinner.

Tino and my grandmother kept seeing each other. She retired after working for forty years at a mental hospital. Tino liked to drive and took my grandmother on many trips. They took me on a trip to Canada when I was two years old. Tino must have been a wonderful person to spend time with for my grandmother who was, after all, a widow living in the town of Ovid, in upstate New York, where there was not a lot of adventure. Tino was full of adventure. He took my grandmother to Rome, Paris, Colorado, and bought her jewelry. They read books and planted flowers together.

My family doesn't know the details of how their relationship began. But when my parents met Tino for the first time, he pulled them aside and said, "There are some things you should know about me...about my past."

My earliest memories of Tino are seeing him with my grandmother on Christmas Eve, when my family would always go to my grandmother's house. He was a short, stocky man with bulging eyes and a wide smile who was always shuffling around the kitchen. He would cook steak sandwiches, make my uncle champagne cocktails, shake my hand with a vice-like grip, and tell stories. He would call me a champion. He bought me my first racing bike with my named engraved on it, played handball with me when I was eight, and wrote me twenty five letters.

In one he wrote,

Dear Pal Jack,

God Bless You, young man. I hope this note finds you doing well in every way possible. Grandpa thinks of you every day and I just want you to know that I cannot wait until the day you reach the age where you have a driver's license; I am going to get you a new Honda.

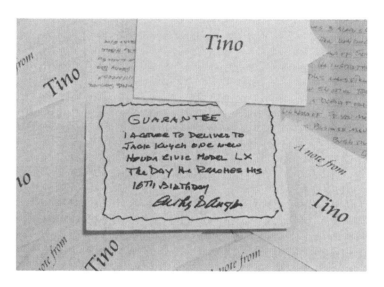

Despite writing in an informal contract: "*Guarantee: I agree to deliver to Jack Knych one new Honda Civic model LX the day he reaches his 16ᵗʰ birthday,*" I never saw the car. But I loved Tino nonetheless, and I didn't mind when he called himself Grandpa Tino. My family loved Tino as well.

But my grandmother's relationship with Tino would be tested in 1992, when the F.B.I. invaded her home to arrest Tino for using $660,000 of forged letters from the Savings Bank of the Finger Lakes to purchase more than $1 million of pork from a Canadian firm. He would be convicted and sent to prison for the third time.

*

In 2010, a year after Tino's death, I was in college pulling an all-nighter for my Financial Economics class. I was reading a book on the history of the stock market, when I came across a chapter on Tino. I almost fell out of my chair. I learned that he had almost caused the stock market to crash in 1963 by committing the most notorious white-collar crime in American history at the time, and that he had been a millionaire in the 1950s and 1960s. I remember thinking, "Was this really the same man who had been in love with my grandmother? Was this the same man who I had a picture of on my dorm room wall, posing ridiculously on an old-fashioned bicycle? And if so, *who was he?*"

The next day I called my father and had the truth of Tino's crimes confirmed. When my father met Tino in 1985, he had been uncertain whether Tino was telling the truth concerning his criminal past, so my father went to the Bird Library at Syracuse University to check the newspaper archives to verify Tino's story. Sure enough, Tino had been on the front of page of *The New York Times* for what called the "Salad Oil Swindle." He had served seven years in federal prison for defrauding his clients for over $150 million (equivalent to $1.2 billion in 2018). For the next eight years I would intermittently research Tino's life, to try and learn more about the man who tried to marry my grandmother.

*

Anthony "Tino" DeAngelis was born in 1915 in the Bronx, the oldest son of Italian immigrants. "Tino" translates to "endearing little fellow of the angels." He grew up in poverty in a cold-water flat with four younger siblings. When interviewed by journalists later in life, Tino would reflect upon his childhood and say, 'I wanted to do one thing in life – make a success. Even as a little kid, I partook very little of the gay life."

Tino quit school at sixteen. Soon after, he borrowed $500 from his father, which he invested in a candy store. The candy store failed.

After the candy store went under, Tino would begin working as a helper at a meat market. One of the stories he would tell my family on Christmas Eve was about when he first saw a bicycle in a store. He told his mother,

"Let's buy it," and convinced the man behind the counter to give him the bike. "My father has a dependable job on the railroad," he told the man. "We'll pay through installments." When Tino left the store with his mother and the bike, his mother said,

"Jesus Christ, Tino, your father is gonna kill me." But Tino paid off the bike.

Within three years of working at the meat market, Tino had risen from helper to manager. By the age of twenty, he was managing two hundred employees.

When asked about being a manager at the age of twenty, Tino would reply, "There were always jealousies and stubbornness. But nothing deterred me. I've always had a brilliant and productive mind."

Tino then became the foreman for the City Provision company, a big hog processing outfit in the Bronx. Thirty years later, people in the meat markets would still remember his exploits with a cleaver.

"I had an exceptional ability in knowing how to process hogs," Tino would say. "Some of my methods, like cutting hogs while they were moving, cut the cost of processing hogs enormously."

In 1938, at the age of twenty-three, Tino opened his own business called M+D Hog Cutters, with $2,000 he had borrowed. Within a year, he was turning a profit of $100,000. Within three years, he was processing three thousand hogs a day and earning a profit of $300,000. Tino pioneered the idea of Western-dressed hogs in the East.

"I never took a vacation, I never went to the racetrack, I never played cards," said Tino. "I worked sixteen hours a day, no one worked harder, on Sunday I stayed home or went to a bicycle meet."

Tino's business exploits would continue to grow. On

November 14, 1955, with $500,000 in capital and with the help of twenty two loyal cohorts, Tino created the Allied Crude Vegetable Oil Refining Company. In the late 1950s, the company was earning annual sales of $200 million.

"No one ever did more for the economy of this country than I did," said Tino.

*

But people were starting to become jealous and suspicious of Tino's success. An assistant vice president of First National City Bank told Norman C. Miller, the author of "The Great Salad Oil Swindle."

"Some people have an ace up their sleeve but Tino has a whole deck of aces. He always seemed to know someone in the right place who could sign a piece of paper or make a phone call or take care of things."

When business would start to falter, Tino would take out more loans. In the early 1960s, he tried to corner the salad oil market because he believed a cartel had formed against him to run him out of business.

"The objective of this clique," Tino said, "was to the put the guinea bastard out of business."

But his attempt to corner the salad oil market would fail, as he engaged in fraud on an unprecedented scale. Through loans from American Express and other banks, Tino would claim that he owned more salad oil than existed in the world at the time. He had been filling salad oil tanks in New Jersey with ninety percent water and sludge. His rational was always: "I'll eventually pay the loans back." When Tino's crimes were discovered, American Express Warehousing, Ltd claimed bankruptcy, and if it wasn't for the assassination of John F. Kennedy three days later, which overshadowed the crime, many believe the stock market could well have crashed.

*

When Tino was arrested at my grandmother's house in 1992, twenty nine years after The Great Salad Oil Swindle, he had opened a company in my grandmother's name, had conducted business in the barn my family built, had threatened a client with suicide, and would be sentenced to twenty one months in federal prison at the age of seventy seven. My grandmother had to testify in front of a Grand Jury. At the time, she thought she was finished with Tino.

But when Tino was released from prison for the third time, he began seeing my grandmother again.

Master Jack Knych

The picture I sent you of the Honda that I was thinking about getting for you may not be to your liking, so you can pick out any color you want – any style you want – or whatever car you want other than the Honda, and Grandpa will get it for you.

You know I love you very much and I can't wait to get up there this summer and have our little game of handball and see how we do against each other. You have to remember that I can't move around as I used to move because of the problems I have with my back.

Meanwhile, I look forward to seeing you and we can take a ride with a bicycle that you have there (which is a real beauty). I think taking a ride in a park where there's not much traffic will make me very happy. Take care.

All my love,
Grandpa Tino

Tino never asked my grandmother to compromise her relationship with her children and grandchildren. And until the day he died on September 26, 2009, at the age of ninety-three, Tino had grandiose plans for business. He always kept a yellow notepad with him, to write down ideas for business ventures. He talked to me often about our opening restaurants together, selling beef that had been aged for months in special refrigerators. Even at the age of ninety, he was planning businesses that would take ten to fifteen years to implement. Tino loved being in the game.

Did my grandmother love Tino? I don't know. When I told her that I was writing a story on Tino, she made it clear that she didn't want to be involved. She said that Tino would never talk about her, so she would never talk about him.

Still, I like picturing my grandmother with Tino, driving across the Canadian countryside with me as a baby in the backseat. Tino, I was told, had bought me a bulk case of bottled milk. I picture him and my grandmother with the windows down, laughing. And I think of one thing my grandmother did let slip about her relationship with him:

"We had a lot of fun."

10.

The Last King
Ashley Okwuosa

W here I'm from, you can choose your name. You can choose the name you will be remembered by, but it comes with a responsibility. My great grandfather's name was Vitus, but the name that resonates with the memory of his life is Ogana Edozie Obi II, which is less of a name and more of a mandate to restore what was once broken in our family. He inherited the name from his father, Okoronkwo, who was Ogana Edozie Obi I. He took the title, and with it the burden, as a way to repair the damage his father and grandfather had wrecked upon the family.

The tale that set things in motion for this story and my family, is the tale of a father and a son. It is about Okoronkwo and his father, Okwuosa ,and the story starts like this: Obua was my great grandfather's great grandfather. Obua's son, Okwuosa was a warrior and fighter in the village of Umutogwuma whose exploits were legendary.

Obua's wife, Nwaketi, was expected to marry Okwuosa after Obua's death. Nwaketi was, according to Igbo tradition, not merely a member of the family, but, in effect, the family's property, which meant that a member of the family had to marry her. Rumor had it, however, that Nwaketi was in love not with Okwuosa, but with his son, Okoronkwo. Defying tradition, Nwaketi married Okoronkwo, causing a rupture between father and son. But there was more to their rift than a wife. Okoronkwo was not at all like his father. Where Okwuosa the warrior was a brash and quarrelsome man, his son, Okoronkwo, was conciliatory and, as such, chose his name and title as a statement of his desire to repair the damage he had helped inflict upon the family.

In fact, wrote my great uncle, the family historian,

Okoronkwo's choice of his name "resulted from a reactionary desire to be completely unlike his father."

"Okoronkwo," he went on, "spent his life trying to mend the wrongs his father perpetrated on people and appeasing the gods for his heartless acts. He liked to be called Edoziobi as an Ogana because he literally built and cleaned the whole Obua and Nwaubani kindred."

Okoronkwo and Nwaketi had five children, among them a son, Vitus, who continued his father's desire to restore the harmony that would make all the warring sides of the family to feel as one. Vitus and his wives, in turn, had thirty six children. One of them was Emmanuel, who would become my grandfather, and who wanted nothing more than to be a leader like them. For a while, he was.

Emmanuel did not seem a likely leader. He was not the oldest, smartest, or most capable of his many brothers. But he longed for the title — "He wasn't the favorite child or son," my father later, his oldest son, told me. "He didn't study to be a doctor or engineer, or didn't really want to be a lawyer. He just wanted to make money. I think he was looking for validation." Validation that would come with a title and with it the responsibility of continuing the restoration of the Okwuosa family.

At eighteen, he was a fan of the British singer Cliff Richards, so much so that his friends nicknamed him Cliff Erisco, a nickname for a flashy young man. He wore corduroy jackets, played the guitar, and was part of a band, The Stella Maris Beach Boys, who sang Beatles covers. In 1963, with Nigeria's independence still tenuous, he was enjoying the highlife and juju music of Ebenezer Obey, Victor Olaiya, and Erasmus Jenewari. But when the country caved in on itself in the midst of civil war and split in half, he went to fight for the breakaway nation of Biafra. It was during the war that he met Patricia, who would become my grandmother.

They married after the war and moved to 18 Okwuosa Street — the street named for his warrior great grandfather. The house sat on one of the plots of land Emmanuel's father had apportioned to his sons. The house would become my father's childhood home, and later mine.

In the years that followed, many things happened. Emmanuel and Patricia had five boys: Major, Hamilton, Hector, Denning and Diamond, in quick succession. In true Erisco fashion, the sons favored bell bottoms, high fades, racerback tanks, and lion print agbada's. They were not the Beach Boys; they were the Jackson Five. Emmanuel was making money. His resume read lawyer, farmer, banker, economic development expert, and global traveler.

When his father died, Emmanuel, seeing his moment, reached out to catch the baton, to become the family's leader. No one disputed his claim. He was a rich man and deemed worthy. But Emmanuel was not content with merely adding another Roman numeral to the titles of his father and a grandfather. He wanted something grander. The young man in the photo known as Cliff Erisco didn't want to be the one who *restored* order to the home. He wanted to be home itself. So he chose the name Obiajie, which means home of the Ajie clan and home of the Okwuosa clan. The title was large and unapologetic. Its mandate was any and everything, and Emmanuel welcomed it.

"That was before he wanted to save the world," said my father of the photo of his father as a young man. "That was him trying to find himself, and hopefully us."

*

In Vitus's autobiographical recollections, he wrote that "children do not merely take after their parents in their physical features. They bear a resemblance to them also in the internal structures that make them who they are." This is true of my grandfather.

By 1976, my grandfather was a newly minted lawyer with a degree from the University of Nigeria and a first time business owner. He began Obiaje Enterprises, a catchall business that was poised to take advantage of Nigeria's burgeoning economy. The business included crop farming, a printing press, and a stream of dairy imports from Europe. The business was so big that twenty years later he estimated that he had raked in close to $5 million in annual sales. Like his father, he had become a success. Vitus had made so much money that when it was made known that he was going away on a trip, a line formed outside his house where he would hand out money to people from the neighborhood.

"People just kept coming," said my father. "They just kept joining the line and he just kept giving."

My grandfather understood that being a man of means was essential to his title of Obiaje. More than making money to have, it seemed that Obiaje made money to give. It was only right. If you were going to be the *home* where the clan gathered, that meant that you would have to be able to hold the family together, literally and figuratively. His house became the meeting place for everyone. People came to him for solutions to their problems. Did someone need their tuition paid? Was someone late on rent? Did a newly married couple need money to jumpstart their life? It seemed as if when he reached into the folds of his *agbada*, he was reaching in the deep pockets for money to give, and when he tapped his fingers — adorned with thick gold rings — he was searching for a solution to your problem. His desire to be of help was a combination of genuine goodwill, and a sense of responsibility, ad hubris.

"He just wanted to be remembered," said my father. "He wanted his family to be remembered."

He named his first son, my father, Major. A spoken wish that, after his death, his son would surpass him in importance. His name for me, which was left off my birth certificate, is Ogbeanu, which loosely translates to mean that I could by no means be betrothed to a man with no wealth. Once, during a routine traffic stop, a police officer asked his driver to produce documentation for his vehicle. The driver, incredulous, asked the officer, "Do you know who the owner of this car is? Do you know who Obiaje is?" The tactic is a common Nigerian one, a way to intimidate by asking someone to recognize your importance — "Don't you know who I am?" But the police officer had no idea who my grandfather was. The shocked driver replied, "You have to meet this man, he will change your life."

That's what my grandfather wanted to do, he wanted to change people's lives. In some ways, it seemed like he wanted to be immortalized in that way so that after his death, his name as Obiaje would speak for him almost asking anyone who cared, "do you know who I am?"

But then, in 1993, the bank my grandfather had led as chairman for almost a decade dissolved. The bank, it turned out, was insolvent and some members of the staff had been accused of fraud. The bank was liquidated, and this shook Obiaje's confidence and left him in a complicated position. As he rose up the ranks in the bank, he had paid less attention to the various streams of income he had nurtured — paper and dairy from Europe and pig farms in eastern Nigeria — and they suffered in his absence. He decided to leave. As it happened, his sons had already left before, and four had settled in Connecticut, and in the spring of 1996 that is where he and my grandmother joined them. The move, however, was not an acceptance of defeat. Rather it was an opportunity for him to plan his triumphant return.

"He bragged and said that when he returned to Nigeria it was going to be an event," said my Uncle IJ, the youngest of his sons.

"Everyone will know."

*

He lived in West Haven, with one of his sons. He traded his black Chevrolet Caprice Classic for a red mountain bike, which he rode around the neighborhood. He also filled his brown Samsonite briefcase with copies of a resume, a one pager that attempted to capture who Obiaje was. But the single page seemed insufficient, and no job fit him quite right.

Obiaje couldn't be anything lesser than Obiaje. Yet in the confines West Haven, no one knew who that was. So, for time being, he settled for being just a father. In hindsight, his sons now recognize that something more was going on. He had stopped taking his medication for high blood pressure, even as he continued to exercise vigorously. Still, in retrospect, his sons now see he was anticipating not his return, but his end. He reminded him always to care for their mother, and to be prudent with their money.

"I never understood that, but he taught me that lesson because he was dying," said my uncle Ken.

*

On a Thursday morning in May of 1996 Obiaje was going to the gym. He declined an offer from his son to drop him off, saying that the air smelled "good and fresh" and he was going to ride his bike. So he rode it for almost twenty minutes to the gym. I can imagine him walking into the gym, getting on the treadmill, and beginning to run, the soles of his sneakers making thudding sounds as it struck the machine belt. The fall was quick but loud. The doctor described it to my uncle as "turning off a light switch." According to a report from Connecticut's Office of the Chief Medical examiner, my grandfather died of Atherosclerotic Coronary Artery Disease, which means that he died from a slow buildup of plaque in his arteries that slowed down the flow of blood to his heart.

My grandfather did have his eventful return home, though not as he had hoped. My uncle describes scores of people arriving at the airport to welcome Obiaje's cold body. Heralded by his sons, Obiaje returned to 18 Okwuosa Street in an ambulance, an ironic vehicle to move a man that was already dead. After the ceremonial funeral rites were performed, four of Obiaje's five sons returned to the leafy suburbs of Connecticut. One, however, stayed behind.

"I felt like I needed to," said my father.

My father assumed his father's position out of necessity and a sense of responsibility. He paid his father's debts, repaired broken relationships and returned to his childhood home at 18 Okwuosa Street.

My father is not the sort of man who draws attention to himself. His father was. My grandfather was showy in his manner and in his generosity. My father gives, but does so quietly. He has become a different sort of leader than his father, just as his father became a different kind of leader than his grandfather, and his grandfather became a different kind of leader than his own father, so long ago.

"He so wanted to keep this whole big family idea going," my father told me. "Obiaje loved ceremony and I don't. I guess I saw too much of it. I didn't set out to do it like he did." He has taken a new title, and it is not Obiaje. Instead he has taken his own name.

"What's bigger than Major?" he said, laughing.

11.

Friend-in-Law
Jennifer Nguyen

M y Great Grandmother Ly was used to being alone. And when her husband died after a tumultuous life of alcoholism, she carried on with her life as a young single mother without any thought of remarrying. She continued tending to her family's coffee and tea plantation by herself. Gossip spreads quickly in the small villages of Laos. And where she lived in Vientiane, the country's capital, was no different. People knew everything about everyone, and it wasn't seen as being nosy -- that's just how things were.

But my great grandmother wanted nothing to do with all of that. Although she was a motherly figure to those in her neighborhood, she didn't engage with anyone below the surface-level pleasantries. She was on her own.

So it was to her surprise that, when her youngest son got married a few years later, she didn't just gain another family member upon meeting her daughter-in-law's mother. She found a best friend.

It has now been fifty years since Great Grandmother Ly and Great Aunt Tu became acquainted. The women went through the diplomatic pleasantries that tend to come with marrying into one another's families. They weren't instant friends -- after all, my great grandmother was always a woman of solitude, and as a widow who was tending to the family's plantation on her own, she usually had her hands full with work with very little time to enjoy a social life. So it wasn't until years later, when they had each immigrated to the United States that they began to spend time together. Great Grandmother Ly, with her children and her grandchildren, stayed at a refugee camp in Guam for three months in 1975, before finally settling in northeast Philadelphia. Great Aunt Tu's family followed shortly after, and both families settled in the outskirts of the city.

My great grandmother, like many Vietnamese at that time, came to America as a political refugee. As the Vietnam War began to worsen and its tumultuous effects were rippling through the rest of Southeast Asia, it wasn't safe for her to stay in Laos, where she and her children lived as ethnic minorities. But the biggest change that came with moving here was that she was no longer obligated to her plantation. By the time she settled herself in Philadelphia, she was considered to be "too old" to start her life over and find work. It didn't help that she didn't speak a breath of English, and she ended up never learning the language during the course of her life. She relied on her children and grandchildren to take care of her, and they were more than happy to oblige, as obedient Vietnamese children were supposed to do.

Her life became much calmer. She could enjoy her days without worrying about how her plantation crops were doing, nor did she have a war to fret over. For the first time in her life, she was at peace. And she was able to enjoy the company around her, which included Great Aunt Tu.

She, too, didn't have to work anymore. She lived with her daughter and spent her days in the company of her grandchildren, also not having to concern herself with whether or not she'd still have a home in Laos. As in-laws who didn't know anyone else in a new, faraway country, Ly and Tu saw each other often during family gatherings. And with the dozens of children and grandchildren between them, those get-togethers happened often, with each cluster of relatives going back and forth from each woman's home.

From the outside, my great aunt didn't seem very similar to my Great Grandmother Ly, despite their both being elderly Vietnamese women who were relatively close in age. Tu and her children had immigrated to the Philadelphia suburbs from the outskirts of Saigon; the twang of her southern Vietnamese accent echoed in every syllable she would speak. Her thin lips were usually curved into a playful smile, always in admiration of her boisterous children, who were constantly surrounding her. Even well into her eighties, she walked with a smooth, lively gait of a woman decades her junior.

Great Grandmother Ly, who was a couple years older than Tu, balanced the friendship with a more pensive air. While Tu was seemingly more outgoing, my great grandmother was much more reserved. Silence always lingered in her presence, but it wasn't an eerie silence. It was a silence of a woman who, even well into her late nineties, found wonder in the new world around her. Her gentle smile reflected her almost childlike ability to find fascination in everything. Having lived such a confined life as a young woman, it was no surprise that the freedom that came with life in America fascinated her.

For the first time in her life, Great-Grandmother Ly had a friend. A friend who was willing to join her on beach-side Atlantic City visits while her children played the slot machines at the casinos. Under large umbrellas, the two women would sit by the shore in beach chairs and breathe in the salt air. When the sun would begin to set, they'd take a stroll, only short ones at a time, for as far as their slow steps could take them.

They'd take other short trips around the country together, whether it was to New York or to Kentucky to visit one of my great uncles. Great Grandmother Ly and Great Aunt Tu saw each other quite often, and they were always side by side, the two matriarchs who, unlike everyone else in the family, could not be bothered with the idle gossip so reminiscent of home.

Great Grandmother Ly's eightieth birthday was one of the few times that the whole Nguyen family was able to gather. My Aunt Nga moved to France in the late 1970s, and so my cousins, Julie and Lien, grew up outside Paris and didn't visit Great Grandmother Ly very often when they were young. And so, when they were visiting Philadelphia during the summer of 1987, it was only natural that our great grandmother's birthday celebration was a bigger occasion than usual.

The day began with the same excitement that usually swirls around the house on party days. All of the aunties arrived early to Uncle Dominic's house in the morning to prepare the food, which typically involves an array of Vietnamese and Laotian dishes -- spring rolls, rice crepes, the usual fare. The house itself is a small one-story home in the Philadelphia suburbs, and all the cooking aromas wafted through the house throughout the day.

My great grandmother, however, stood back from the cooking. She kept trying to go into the kitchen, peeking through the doorway with her worried eyes to see what she could do. My grandmother, who, as the only daughter in her family, was Great Grandmother Ly's caretaker by default. She pushed her mother away from the kitchen and blocked the doorway.

"Don't worry about it! Just go sit on the couch and relax," she said as she shooed away Great Grandmother Ly.

My great grandmother was used to being a busybody. But not just any old busybody -- she was an incredibly independent busybody. She raised her children all on her own after her alcoholic husband died when they were very young. She tended to the plantation on her own, with no help from anyone else. Everything she did, she did all by herself. And so when her daughter and daughters-in-law were taking it upon themselves to plan the birthday party, my great grandmother didn't know what to do with herself. Despite the fact that she was turning eighty years old, she still had a quickness to her step, even if sometimes her aging body wouldn't keep up the way she'd want it to. She constantly had to move, and she badly wanted to be in the kitchen to take control.

Slightly dejected, she resigned herself to sitting on the couch. Great Aunt Tu was already sitting there, watching the great grandchildren play in the living room, and watching television. After maybe the third attempt to go into the kitchen, Great Grandmother Ly sat down next to my great aunt. They exchanged a smile and joked about how they both weren't allowed to help out with the party, turning back to the little ones and their toys. As the night carried on, their conversation drifted to their lives in Laos, adjusting to America, and how ridiculous their children were as they tried to outdo each other with money and material extravagances.

After dinner was over, the tables were cleared as the aunties brought out two birthday cakes. My grandmother, concerned that the modest Swiss mocha cake wasn't enough, made her son run out to quickly pick up a sheet cake. Great Grandmother Ly and Great Aunt Tu were facing the cakes, the birthday candles glowing and their young great grandchildren excitedly jumping around behind them.

Great Grandmother Ly, however, wasn't overly thrilled, and just sat there quietly and took everything in. She was never someone who craved attention. If she had things her way, she would've been back on that couch, sitting with Tu, chatting about the good old days in Laos and avoiding the birthday celebration.

A young life of solitude and distance from the rest of the world meant that birthdays were unimportant to my great grandmother. So unimportant, in fact, that no one knew when she was actually born, not even her own children. For the sake of simplicity, her birthday was celebrated on July 4th -- the same day as her daughter's birthday. No one ever questions it, or thinks it's odd that there's no memory of when Great Grandmother Ly's birthday actually was. It just was.

As the rest of the family sang happy birthday to her, she looked calmly at the cake. She appreciated the effort her in-laws and children had put into her day, especially her daughter, who didn't mind ceding the celebration of her own birthday to mark her mother's eightieth year. When the singing stopped, my grandmother motioned for the children to come closer to help Great Grandmother Ly blow out the candles. They ran up, but were unable to reach the table.

"Just do it yourself, Ly," Great Aunt Tu said, glancing over to my great grandmother. "It'll be okay."

But then Great Grandmother Ly moved to San Jose.

*

My grandmother didn't want to live in Philadelphia anymore. And wherever my grandmother went, Great Grandmother Ly had to go, too. An aunt who lived in California offered them place in her house. Her husband was gone on business in China for most of the year, and she could use the help tending to her own younger children, who were then just toddlers. A change of scenery was enticing, and so in 1998, my great grandmother said goodbye to everyone, including Great Aunt Tu, and left for the west coast.

As Great Grandmother Ly got older, traveling back and forth became increasingly more difficult. Not even a wheelchair could make it easier. In the last few years of her life, she stopped visiting family in Philadelphia, and thus stopped seeing her friend.

The concept of calling Great Aunt Tu on the phone wasn't an option for my great grandmother. She lived most of her life not knowing how to use a phone, so it didn't even occur to her that it was something that she could do. They spoke little in the years that preceded Great Grandmother Ly's death in 2005 in San Jose.

I remember the last time I saw her before she died. She was ninety eight years old and her memory was nearly gone. By then, she and my grandmother had moved to a senior condominium in town, and Great Grandmother Ly spent most of her days sitting in the dark living room by herself, confined to the couch unless my grandmother was able to help her. This summer day was no different.

My mom pushed me in front of my great grandmother, who was seated on a reclining chair, with blankets draped over her lap.

"Do you know who this is?" my mom asked Great Grandmother Ly.

She looked up at me with twinkling eyes.

"Ahh, it's Ngoc Quynh," Great Grandmother Ly said my Vietnamese name in a cheerful voice.

Great Aunt Tu died a few years later, having remained behind in Philadelphia. She spent her final years with her children and grandchildren. But as it was with my great grandmother, friendless.

12.

She's the Girl
Pragya Krishna

My parents' marriage is so weird that I still kind of look at it and go, "huh?" They say it's a product of time and circumstance, which sounds very Zen, except that they don't act at all Zen about it and they never have.

To me, it looks like two kids who didn't even know each other got married because that's what they were supposed to do, and they've been stuck ever since in the aftermath of a choice they were not equipped to make.

My mom was twenty three, three years younger than I am now. She says she's an "unconscious" kind of person and always has been. It makes me think of a plant or a snail or one of those rock-like sea creatures that just stays in place until something prods it to move.

She came home one day and saw the house was, in her words, "all decorated." She was in her final year of medical school, in the middle of her final exams. She'd just pulled an all-nighter, there was another exam the next day, and she was surprised.

She went in and put her bag down. The house was in Lucknow, India, where my mother's medical college was. Her father was in the revenue services, which is a government career with postings that change every few years, so her parents were living in another city where he'd been assigned. She was staying with her older brother and his wife in the family home. She had three older sisters, who'd all been married off, but she hadn't really thought about the possibility that she was next.

When her brother's wife saw she'd come home, she said, "Pinky [my mom's nickname], take an hour to rest and then get dressed up. There's a boy coming to see you."

"And I was so angry," my mother recalls. "I said I don't want to meet anyone. I had no decent clothes, I'd put on weight because I'd been binge-eating *parathas* because of the stress from studying. I was like, my hair's like this, I don't want to meet anyone."

But after her outburst, she calmed down and obeyed, in accordance with her nature. She listened to her parents in all things, and these *were* her parents' directions by proxy. "I said fine, and we started looking through my wardrobe. I found an old *dhoti*-type suit and I said, I'll wear this."

The boy arrived soon after and sat down in the living room. He had come with a friend. "I didn't even know which one of them was the boy in question," my mother says.

She went on autopilot. Guests are supposed to be treated with courtesy, so she acted accordingly. "Someone's come to the house, I'm supposed to be an attentive hostess and be nice. 'Please, have these *rasgullas*. I insist.'"

The young man in question, she says, had thought he didn't want to marry a doctor. His friend, who was known to be tactless, said to her, "What if you were asked to forget you're a doctor after marriage?"

She bristled.

The young man, however, intervened and said to his friend, "What kind of question is that? How would you feel if you were asked to forget you're a scientist?"

"So then I thought, alright," she says. "The guy has good sense."

The rest of the conversation was just small talk, and when it was done my mom went back to her room and forgot about the whole thing. The young man came back later and picked up some pictures of her -- a common practice during the arranged marriage process. "I didn't know about it at the time," my mother told me. "I was back to studying again. I paid no attention."

But then, she says, "Exams were done, and my brother was like, okay, now you're getting married."

*

Hang on, I say to her. When did the exams end and when was the engagement?

The engagement was June 21. The wedding was to be a

week later.

The exams were at the end of May. So what happened in those three weeks?

"Nothing," she says. She and the young man did not speak at all. "I went to Jabalpur to stay with my parents."

*

"The story really starts with Ram Samujh, from the '81 batch," my father says.

A little explanation here. My dad's in the revenue services. These are a branch of the Indian Civil Services, which are a holdover from colonial times and *extremely* difficult to get into -- the current success rate is 0.03 percent. Social interaction among those in the civil service functions rather like an old boys' network. Hearing people identify each other by their "batch" -- the year they qualified, is normal. My dad's of the '86 batch.

Once you pass the exam, you go to the training academy of the service you've been selected for. That's where my dad met Ram Samujh. "Ram Samujh was posted there too, as an assistant director of investigation. He belongs to our caste." We come from a Scheduled Caste family, one of the most historically oppressed castes in India -- so activism and connections on that basis are main determining factors in social life.

Ram Samujh took it upon himself as a mentor to introduce my father to prospective wives. "He said, there's someone I know, he's posted in Jabalpur as a deputy commissioner. He has a daughter that he's looking to find a match for. I replied that I was appearing for the civil services again to try for a different service and I wasn't interested at this time."

I break in with a different question. "What about that whole phase where you thought you'd take a vow of celibacy for the rest of your life?"

"Well, that was in college. I hadn't converted to Buddhism at the time," he replies. "But the *Kabir Panth* had a lot of influence on me." The *Kabir Panth* is an Indian system of philosophy, not religious, emphasizing rationalism, very similar to Buddhism. "You know, with concepts like, relationships and attachments are lies…"

He was so committed to the idea that he began fasting. "That was in my final year of college, I found this book on *ayurveda* and there was no one to tell me I was being misguided. It had couplets I still remember:
Don't desire for tea, don't look for coffee,
Lemon in warm water, over all ills will give you victory
But we digress.

"I'd also read and seen plenty about how much getting involved with girls was distracting," he says. "So I was really strict about controlling that desire by always looking at the ground while I walked, not making eye contact with girls because that's how attraction starts."

My father, however, was a very good catch; literally everyone who passes the civil services exam is pounced on, even now. It's like a meat market. So it was that one night an older man came to the door. He was carrying a small briefcase and a packet of sweets, and said that he had been referred by Ram Samujh. "I have a daughter," the man said. "I'd like to get her married to you."

"I was in a fix," are my dad's exact words. "I excused myself, went inside and told my roommate, can you tell him I don't want to get married. My roommate said, the man has come from so far by flight -- in those days, flights were very costly -- it would be rude to just say no outright. You can refuse him later, but at least listen to him for politeness' sake."

So my dad went back out into the living room and sat and talked with the man for half an hour. The man rose to leave and said, "If you want to, and if you feel like it, let us know." He left his address and phone number. He also made a point of saying that his daughter really liked village life and that he himself was from a village.

But almost immediately after meeting the man a problem arose. A classmate knew the family and warned my father against a match. "Don't marry that man's daughter, she's not good," he told my father. "That entire family is not good, I know them. And that particular girl is a drama queen, and I remember her doing a stage performance and playing the role of a eunuch."

In the meantime, the man's son sent him a picture of the girl. Actually, of the girl and her sisters. The brother had drawn a circle around the girl's face as well as an arrow pointing to her.

My dad showed it to his roommate and asked what he should do. Send it back, the roommate replied. So he did, without comment.

In the months following, however, he got violently ill, which allowed his friends to admonish him about continuing to live as a bachelor, subsisting on hotel food.

I have to ask: "So basically, they said you should get married so you could have a cook?"

He replies, "No, it was also about having company."

"Now there was a *different* proposal for the daughter of another official, who lived in Lucknow," he says. "He'd been calling me a lot, and everyone was telling me what a good man he was. I'd been putting him off, but he was insistent. So I said, okay, let's go meet them."

He and his friend visited the family. "The girl was alright," he says. "But...and maybe this was just my sexism which I wasn't aware of at the time...we'd sat down to lunch, and she was finished before I was, and she turned to her mom and said, 'Mom, I'm sleepy. Can I go take a nap?' And her mother said yes, go."

"We hadn't even spoken," my dad says. "I thought, if she doesn't even have the patience to sit through a lunch, how will she have the patience to adjust with my family? As we were leaving, her mother said, 'So, son, when are you going to the village? Should we go talk to your family?' and I answered right there, 'I'm sorry, ma'am, but I don't think this will work out.'"

He and his friend were about to head home when his friend reminded him of the man referred by Ram Samujh who had come to visit. "Don't they live nearby?"

"I thought, oh yeah, they live right in front of Lucknow University. I was like, you're right, since we're here, why not meet them?"

"But then I thought, I don't even know if they're home. It wasn't planned, I hadn't kept their numbers. So I called

Ram Samujh, and he said, sure, write down the number." So he called and introduced himself.

"I'm visiting Lucknow, should I drop by? And he said, of course, come to our house."

"The first thing that struck me was her voice," my father says. "I was like, it's sweet like a nightingale's." My mom does have a nice voice. "We didn't talk a lot, I was just observing her." Then his careless friend asked what she did and made his stupid 'What if you were told to forget you were a doctor?' comment. "I thought it was such an awkward and moronic thing to say. It's one thing to ask, 'would you choose career over family?' But to say it like that, I turned to him and said 'What kind of brainless question is that? What if you were told to forget you've done an M.Sc.?' and he shut up."

The girl said nothing in response. She just picked up a plate of snacks the servant had brought, extended it toward my father and said, "You haven't eaten anything."

"And I thought, oh wow, this girl is so responsible."

I say, so basically, you made an entire picture in your head of who she was, based on that one sentence, seriously, and my dad laughs and says, yeah, like you said, I was stupid. "I thought, okay, she might be able to handle the responsibility of marriage. My thinking was, her brother was there, her servant was there, she could've left it to them, but she was the one who said, 'Please, I insist.'"

"And I made up my mind right there. 'She's the girl.'"

*

My father had indicated his interest and though the engagement was not official my mother's mother went to see him in Ahmedabad, where his own mother had joined him after he'd gotten so sick.

They had arrived at dawn. My father was still sleeping and so ignored the doorbell. "Then it rang again," he says, "And then three times. I remember thinking, the milkman rings once, the newspaper man rings once, who rings three times?"

Since summer is so hot in India, he was just in a sleeveless undershirt and a *lungi,* which is something like a cross between a sarong and a skirt and is traditional wear for that weather. "I got up, rubbing my eyes, and opened the door to see a short woman with a purse and a man. I just said, 'How can I help you?' and she said 'I'm Mrs. Lal,' and in my head, I was like, who? But clearly they were guests so I let them in and asked them to sit, but I didn't know who they were."

After sitting down in the living room, the lady said, "I'm her mother." My dad thought, whose mother? Then she added, "I'm from Jabalpur."

"And I was like ohh! Mrs. *Puncham* Lal (Lal is an extremely common surname.) So we just sat and chatted and an hour had passed when I realized I hadn't even brushed my teeth."

He told them he'd just go and brush and wash his face, and he did and put on a proper pair of *kurta* and *pajamas.* "The most embarrassing thing," he says, "is I didn't wear underwear when I slept, and your mom still laughs about the incident and says, "What if your *lungi* had unraveled?" I don't know if I was just really foolish or really innocent or really sleepy. I'd been talking to them for an hour without combing my hair or washing my face, and I probably still had sleep grit in my eyes."

In the meantime, his mother had made food for everyone. Afterward, my mother's mother said, "I've come to 'confirm the relationship.' When can you marry my daughter?"

He replied, "It's up to you." So she was the one who fixed the date, for June 27, 1989.

She also set the engagement date for a week before. After that, she left. "She also gave me something like two thousand or three thousand rupees as a 'blessing.' It's called a *roka*. And it effectively means from now on, you're not going to look at relationships with any other girl. You are booked."

From Ahmedabad she traveled to my father's village to meet his family. When she finally arrived home she told my mother, "He's good. A little skinny, but he's light-skinned. I also did the *roka*, I gave him a thousand rupees."

My mom says, "I was just like 'okay'. I was so unconscious. It was as if they were talking about someone else."

As the engagement approached, my father asked a friend, what do you take to an engagement? The friend replied, a good *sari* and a ring. My father says, "I was like, *sari*, really? And he was like, yeah, you can buy one from here in Ahmedabad. So I went to a *sari* shop where he could get me a discount, and bought one for 1,300 rupees. She still has it and wears it to some events, it was from Kala Niketan."

Then he went to Lucknow and asked his friend there to help him buy a ring. "And that's how the engagement happened."

*

In the lead-up to the wedding, my mother continued to remain disconnected from her own life. "I didn't really register that I was getting married. I wasn't prepared. It wasn't that I didn't want to get married ever, I did find boys attractive, but I thought, oh yeah, I might have a few boyfriends, I'll travel. But I also believed in everything my parents said, in all things."

She pauses for a moment, then adds, "Actually, I must have said something to my father, because I remember him saying 'Oh you know, you don't have to get married, it's not a big deal. Chandravati didn't get married either, you don't have to.' Chandravati was a professor at my medical school."

Her eyes go distant and she says, "Chandravati began circling my head," as I try very hard not to laugh. "I thought, oh my god, I don't want to end up like her, she's gone mad from being an old maid."

She thought also of another "old maid" she'd known, her math teacher in tenth grade. "She was so strange and frustrated too, and always shouting at us, venting that frustration. I thought, god, if I don't get married, I'll grow old and frustrated, too. I thought, I'm not smart enough to make it on my own, and I won't even have a family. So I said, okay, okay, I'll get married."

In the middle of all this my father took a risk: he called to speak to her. My mother's father picked up. My father introduced himself. Her father said, "What do you want?" My mom speculates that her father, who could be brusque, didn't want to let them talk and risk having the young man change his mind.

My father, she says, "freaked out and put the phone down."

My mom virtually sleep-walked all the way through the engagement, and then all the way through the wedding itself. "I had no emotion. It was like someone told me, dress like a bride, so I did. All I felt was uncomfortable and hot." It was North India in peak summer, after all.

After the *phere,* the ritual of walking around the fire seven times -- she went back to her room, because in their tradition the bride and groom aren't supposed to be alone together until the bride leaves the house in the *bidaai,* the seeing-off ceremony. "I went back, took off all the heavy jewelry and clothes and just fell soundly asleep. It was like someone else had gotten married. And then the next day they tell me, it's time for the *bidaai,* now go."

This was when the penny finally dropped.

She imitates the words as they sounded to her, as if they suddenly came out of nowhere. The closest example I can think of is when someone is really absorbed in a video game, and you say something to them, and they absently say, "Yeah. Yeah. Uh-huh," until something finally get through, and they're like, "Wait, what?"

"'Now go.' And I was like, I don't want to go anywhere!"

*

My father's memories of the wedding are of being very tired and there being a power outage and having to get dressed in his elaborate wedding costume in a bus by flashlight. "I remember I really had to use the bathroom," he says. His friend told him, "stay in your seat, it'll be over soon. It was over at 2 a.m. I ran to the bathroom as soon as it was done."

The power had come back on by that point, and they'd made arrangements for everyone on my dad's side to stay at a hotel nearby. "So we just went there and slept. I didn't talk to your mother at all."

Meanwhile, my grandparents took my mother back home and told my father that the *bidaai* would be at 8 in the morning.

At 8 a.m. the next day, the groom's party was all there. My dad recalls, "She came out of the house at first, and suddenly burst out, 'I don't want to go.' She started crying and said to her mother, 'Why did you get me married?' and she stomped back inside. We were all so shocked. Your *nani* [my mother's mother] said, just wait a minute, I'll talk to her."

He heard her mother say, "You won't listen to your own mother?" and then they were out of his range of hearing. "I don't know what transpired after that but it was about an hour before they were able to convince her, and make her understand that she'd come back, and then she agreed to come."

How did he feel? "I was upset and it was emotional." My dad tends to cry when other people are crying and *bidaais* are basically waterworks everywhere. "I was thinking, this wedding has happened after so much difficulty, and now she's saying, I don't want to go. And her parents are telling me, she's naive, we'll make her understand."

"She came out for the second time and she was still crying, and I was getting teary-eyed too, and I said to her parents, You don't have to worry, I'll look after her. She's my responsibility now. She's your daughter but she's also my wife."

Which is just as my mother remembers it. "I liked hearing that -- 'She's my wife. I'll look after her.' When he said that, I was like, alright, and I felt okay about going with him."

They left together, in the customarily-decorated car with a driver, in which they didn't speak at all for a while. My mother says, "We were both scared and curled up on opposite sides. It was a two-hour trip, and we didn't even look at each other for most of it. I needed something from my vanity box on the way and I couldn't get the lid to open, so I asked him all timidly, 'Can you open this?' and he did and that was our first real interaction in our marriage."

What was going through my father's head at the time? "I was kind of in shock. It was like a setback I couldn't recover from. I was thinking, I hope it's not that she doesn't even like me, did she not want to get married? I wasn't sure how to behave, what to say, what not to say, how to console her, how to make her comfortable. And I was also just so exhausted, it was like, let me just lie down on the spot and go to sleep."

*

My mother smiles a little, returning to the present for a moment, to the 52-year-old woman who's been married for 28 years; who's spent more of her life with my dad than she has without him, who yells at him when he gets his stomach upset again because he ate something he knows he can't handle even as she takes care of him; whom he tells all his work politics that are still incomprehensible to me; whom he compliments teasingly, tongue-in-cheek every day because she's heard how pretty she is every day of her life since she was born and feels childishly uncomfortable if she goes for too long without hearing it.

"Your dad was already very attached," she says. "He had this perfect world in his head, and all these ideas about how much he'd care for me, and how much I would in return as his wife. For him, this entire thing was very important, but for me, it was an act done in unconsciousness."

In that awkward state, they got to my dad's village, which in their tradition, was now my mother's "real" home. "His family had made preparation for the *muh dikhayi*." A *muh dikhayi*, which literally means "the showing of the face" is a ceremony meant to introduce the bride to the new home. She is veiled and everyone comes one by one to lift it and look at her face and then leave a gift.

"And your dad told them no. Mainly because he was anti-dogma and anti-superstition in a very dogmatic and religious village, but he also said it'd be too stressful for me. It was mid-afternoon in late June, and he really had gone all-out with arrangements, there was a big cooler running, everything was comfortable, and I was tired so I just took a nap." In lieu of the *muh dikhayi,* the ladies of the house just came in one by one to glance at her while she was asleep.

In the evening, she says, "There was really good food, and then at night they'd made sleeping arrangements for us on the terrace, there was a view of a nearby pond and eucalyptus trees everywhere, but we were both so tired that we only slept."

The next day they went back to my mother's house as part of another ceremony, and then they had to take a train to Ahmedabad because my dad had to be back at the office.

"I was so happy to be back with my mom. I asked him, because I was basically a dumb kid, 'Hey, can I go sleep in my sisters' room?' And he was like, 'okay,' and so I went and gave it no thought, just laughing and being silly with my sisters as always, and he was alone and unhappy because that was not how he had expected me to be."

Another term my mom uses to describe herself, apart from "unconscious", is "practical" -- by which she means not sentimental or sensitive.

She tells me, "I had no idea that could hurt him, and for a long time after I found out, I wondered, why does he get hurt over the littlest things?"

*

The photograph that sticks in my mind and which prompted the telling of this story is of the two of them on horses, a moment they'd always referred to as their "honeymoon." It turns out that was an impromptu trip they took six months after their wedding which they really enjoyed and which they refer to as a "honeymoon," but the actual honeymoon was different. "It was right after the wedding, we went to Udaipur and Mount Abu...and your *daadi* [my father's mother] came with us," my mom says.

I don't even know how to explain that because it's another one of those "my family is weird" things that, probably in taking after my mom, I just kind of accept because examining it doesn't feel worth the effort. The best explanation, I think, is that honeymoons are a Western concept, and they're from a generation where the traditional family was fading and everything was shifting. Of his parents, my dad has said, "I never even knew them to sleep in the same room."

So there they were, going on a honeymoon. My mom says, "In the car, it was literally me sitting between your father and your grandmother. We have photos of that trip, too. And then when we got there, your grandmother was confused about why there were two rooms. She said, why are you wasting money, this is a big room, let's get another bed in here." My mom and I dissolve in laughter at this point.

Once I've calmed down, just to send me into another round of giggles apparently, she adds, "Also, on the way your dad was feeling all romantic so he was singing songs, and your grandmother was surprised because she'd only ever seen him as very serious and studious, and she said, 'He's become the kind of person who sings!'"

Returning to her "practical" nature though, my mom continues: "But Udaipur was nice, there were a lot of monuments, and forts. As for our relationship at that point...we still weren't comfortable, we didn't understand anything. And then we came back to Ahmedabad."

They argued a lot, "like children, honestly," says my mother. "There was a park where couples used to hang out and hold hands and that was considered really bold, so we decided we should go there and hold hands too, and ended up arguing about the details of hand-holding."

There was also the time he was offended, she said, because she used the word *tum*, which is an informal Hindi word for "you," instead of the more formal *aap*, and was mimicking him as she was wont to do with her siblings. "He said husbands are not supposed to be mocked. 'A husband is a husband.' We argued about that and came home angry."

She's only ever called him *aap* in my memory.

But they also began to bond. "There was a day when we took a bus to Gandhinagar [a neighboring city] and spent a whole day just sitting under a tree and talking about our lives. We'd shop together, and every day we'd bring in something new, curtains, furniture, and slowly set up the house. It was fun." I'd just set up my new dorm room a few months ago, I said, so I could relate. My mom just looked amused.

But despite that, she says, "Even then, I'd always keep thinking about when I could go back to my mom. And then we had you. May 1991. I'd also started my medical internship in Ahmedabad by that point, and you had come. After that, I became much more comfortable, and my attachment to my parents' home decreased. That was when I really felt this home is my home.

"I will say this, though," she adds. "Despite all the weird unconsciousness with which I went into this marriage, I never once felt, looking at him, who is this? He was never a stranger to me. Even arguing wasn't like arguing with a stranger. And I've never once thought, why did I get married to him? Or even why did I get married?"

*

My father says that when my mother walks with her sisters she walks in step with them. But not so with him. "I don't know if it's a psychological thing. She's always striding ahead. The idea of just a family strolling together, we've never had that. That's what I meant when I said the initial wear-and-tear of marriage had started."

He was referring to how they'd both talked about the photo that prompted these conversations.

My mother had said, "We were comfortable by this point, it was like hanging out with a friend."

My father had said, "It was great, it was the most carefree I've ever been. It was a stage when we were bonding, but the initial wear-and-tear of marriage had started."

126

*

Six months after their wedding -- and the honeymoon they spent with my grandmother – my parents took their first trip alone as a couple. They did not plan an itinerary, and nor did they call my mother's parents, who later made clear their disappointment at not being informed. Their journey took them to a hill station called Nainital, or Lake Naini.

My mom remembers the day as "lightly cold, slightly warm?"

My dad said the weather was clear, though "a little cold. I think there was light fog."

They stayed for a week and my father admits he was a little shy because he had never traveled alone with a girl. He arranged for a romantic dinner – chicken and champagne. But the champagne made my mother so sick she threw up.

One day they hired a guide and horses and it was on that day, at that moment, that this photograph of my mother and father was taken.

"We're totally acting," my dad says, recalling how he pointed into the distance as he sat on his horse. "I'm like, look there. There's nothing there. I mean, it's a mountain, there must've been something there but it was really just a pose.

"There were these really narrow mountain paths with valleys on either side and we were just racing each other to see who could go faster and the poor tour guide was running behind us, asking us to slow down or stop and we didn't listen. It was like that the entire time. We were like a pair of free birds."

13.

Denial
Bianca Heyward

M emory is an act of perception, but when summoned, my memory provides bullshit. I was eight when this photograph was taken, and all I remember of that time was that I adored the two older brothers I am layered between: Bobby, who was fifteen at the time, and Michael, who was thirteen. And they treasured me.

I recall almost nothing more, even amidst the chaos that was swirling around me.

There is so much I don't remember. I don't remember how much my parents struggled, because I had no knowledge of it. The year was 2001.

I do remember my dad walking me to elementary school every morning, and my mom tucking me into bed every night. I used to go swimming with Michael sometimes after school; a gift of living in Los Angeles. I remember having nightmares that would wake me up, propel me out of my bedroom, and downstairs to Bobby's room. He sometimes woke up after I crawled into bed with him and put his arms around me.

But sometimes he wasn't there. I don't really remember.

Bobby and I were seven years apart. He was in high school when I was learning to tie my shoelaces. He joined the golf team at Beverly Hills High School when he was fourteen, but I don't recall it being a big part of his life. That was a year before this photo was taken. I didn't know the coach tested him for drugs. I didn't know what drugs were. I do, however, remember the smell of cigarette smoke. Bobby smoked and I knew that smoking was bad because I overheard my mother and father screaming at him when he smelled of tobacco. Smoking meant punishment.

I have no memory of Bobby being expelled in ninth grade.

This is what I do remember: Bobby was gone for a little

bit. He was sent away. All I remember from when he was away is my mother crying. I'm not sure I was ever told why he had to go, or where he went. But to this day, I can conjure an image of my mother; sitting on the stairs, crying endlessly every day. I know I sat beside her. My cheeks were dry, and hers were wet.

It's strange, though. I know I wrote him letters while he was gone because I have found the ones I received in response. Scribbled, dated, signed, "I love you, Bobby." They resurfaced a few years ago when I was rummaging through my mother's dresser drawers.

Bobby was sent away to a school as punishment. I never knew exactly why, though. He did something bad, and my parents were punishing him. We had dinner as a family five nights a week. I couldn't say exactly how long he was gone. Surely, I would have noticed an empty chair.

Where was I when things had stopped making sense for everyone else around me? Why don't I remember the beginning of Bobby's spiral, and how my parents didn't know what to do?

And why now, at the age of twenty-five, do I finally want to know?

I wanted to understand Bobby and make meaning out of what happened to him, and to us. This photograph sits next to my bed. For my whole life, I have loved him.

*

This year, I asked my mother how long Bobby was gone. When she began to reply, I could see her again, crying on the stairs. Somewhere between seven and ten days, she told me. I made a point of asking her in the middle of the day, mindful of not upsetting her too late at night.

My father confirmed this. But why, I asked him, why was he sent away?

My father told me Bobby had been a good athlete but that he had to push him. He enjoyed playing on the golf team, but lost interest and skipped practice. Then his drug test showed up positive.

He remembers the night Bobby was taken away and how two big men came to the house. He told Bobby that these men were taking him away to a place where he could get off drugs. My father told Bobby he had five minutes to pack his things. My mother remembers packing for him. The men bound his wrists.

And they just took him? I asked.

I thought he'd be safe, he replied. *He didn't cry.*

He didn't scream? I asked.

Then, I said, I have letters from him. Do know want to see them? He wrote, "Listen to Mom and Dad. Tell everyone I love them."

Bobby was expelled from Beverly Hills High in ninth grade. I pushed back on this fact during our conversations. *No he wasn't. What are you talking about? How is it possible I never knew that?*

My parents couldn't believe I was unaware. They both asked me: How could you not know?

My parents, through no fault of their own, did not know what to do at that time.

*

I couldn't accept the gaps in my memory; it seemed inconceivable to my parents and now to me that I never knew any of this. My therapist explained that their surprise is quite significant. As an eight year old, the best I could do was say to myself, "Bobby did something bad, and now he's being punished." Unless my parents sat me down and tried to explain drugs in a way I could understand, there would be no way for me to have comprehended what was obvious to an adult. Bobby was their priority. I was not a problem.

She compared me to children who grow up in war zones. Early on, she explained, I developed survival mechanisms. I created a barrier to block out everything that felt scary or overwhelming. I may have heard things that were frightening or confusing, but I didn't make them a part of my life. I removed myself. Bobby remained the brother I idolized.

This was easy at the time. Bobby and I didn't go to the

same school, and or have the same friends. We were both close with our mother. Michael and I used to joke that Bobby was her favorite.

I have no memory of asking my mother if there was something I could do to help. Instead, I just tried to be the best-behaved child I could, thinking that might make her happy when she sat crying on the stairs.

I convinced myself that Bobby was fine. I had swallowed that myth as a truth. At twenty-five, I have realized I was still in denial. I didn't fully understand until recently just how *not* fine Bobby was. In time, my denial slid into hopelessness—because I was, and always had been—powerless to make things better.

I can't stop digging and looking for answers in order to find out what was going on the moment the camera shutter opened for a split second and captured us in the photograph that sits in a frame next to my bed.

For my whole life, these are the brothers I've loved. Now, I feel I am left here. I have no choice but to tell this fucking story, and I needed a professional to make it clear that it's not at all clear that revisiting the past will make the present any more comprehensible. With each passing day, my memory becomes fuzzier. Sometimes, I need a photo to remind me what Bobby's face looked like.

Bobby died from an accidental drug overdose fifteen years after this photo was taken. He took his last breath in my childhood bed, at the age of thirty, on Father's Day. It was June 21, 2015.

I have come to learn why I have no memory of that time. But I struggle to understand why my brother had to die. I don't understand why he remains frozen in time, captured in a black and white image that sits on my bedside table.

14.

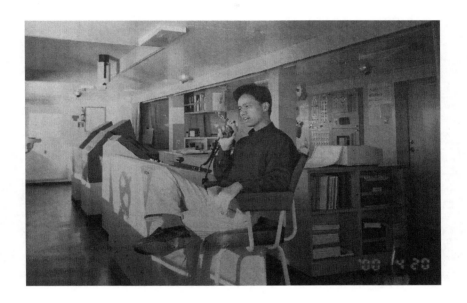

The Sailor's Wife
Momo Hu

E very time Dad came home, the place was different.
The studio where we lived on the second floor of an
old building felt even tinier because a folding metal
frame bed would be pulled out for me and a chair would be
placed for Dad at the dining table. He was not home often,
so the bed and chair were usually packed away and I got
used to sleeping next to Mom and listening to her bedtime
stories. But Dad brought back some good stuff too; every
time he came back I got gifts. There were pink Hello Kitty
pens from Japan, which I brought to school to make more
friends with. There was a thermos that worked so much
better than the water bottles we could find locally.

As the only kid in the family living in a world of my
own, I didn't pay much attention to what Dad brought back
to Mom as souvenirs or gifts when he came back from his
months-long journeys at sea. But I am sure there must have
been many. I now think maybe it is a little unusual that we
received gifts instead of spending time together as a family.
The fact that he was a sailor also makes me feel a little bit
special now -- it's such an ancient profession and the
Chinese were exploring the world in their treasure fleets
centuries before Magellan. But my Dad wasn't on a court
mission bringing back spices or soap for the royal and the
rich, but shipping thousands of kilograms of potato chips
from China to France and bringing tons of chemical
fertilizers back from Germany. And on those long voyages
he would remember to pick up a gift or two for his family,
which was neither royal nor rich.

For most of my childhood my father was gone. It didn't
bother me that much. I only found it funny when he couldn't
recall which grade I was in, and went to the wrong
classroom for one of the very few parent-teacher conferences
he attended. I also laughed at Dad for not being able to make

a decent cup of milk with the powdered milk he brought back from overseas; it was either too thick or too watery. That was when I was in kindergarten, when we were still living in that second floor studio. I would drink a mug of milk made perfectly by Mom every night before I went to bed, listening to her reading a bedtime story. There was Goldilocks and the Three Bears. There was Pippi Longstocking. Later that year when Dad came back, Mom insisted that he make me the bedtime milk.

"Too watery, I can't even taste the milk," I said.

Dad would make another one, with Mom watching and waiting. Then he made another one. Then one more. I am not sure if I was enjoying seeing Dad try and fail and make such an effort for me so that I was being intentionally picky back then. I had so much milk that my nose bled the next day at the kindergarten. Mom said it's because milk is considered "heaty" food.

Now as I look back on it, I think Mom was perhaps aware of my little "scheme" of over-exercising Dad when he was making the milk. But she was just watching, smiling, giving some instructions, and didn't stop Dad from making another cup. Maybe it's because she could understand that I was being a bit demanding when Dad finally was there. Maybe she thought it was important that Dad demonstrate some effort in child rearing when he was home.

In all that time when my father was away, I actually never thought about what was going through my mom's mind, how she felt. There were a lot of New Years and holidays with just Mom. It was Mom who took me to the hospital when I was sick and bought Bugles to cheer me up. It was Mom who taught me how to read and use a dictionary to look up the characters I didn't know yet. It was Mom who put me on the backseat of an old bicycle and rode me to kindergarten and elementary school every morning, until she became too busy with her book or graduate studies in education and hired someone. It was Mom who asked me if I'd like to learn a musical instrument when I was four. (Dad said she made me "learn too many things" when I was little.) It was Mom who went with me to violin lessons every Saturday before I was old enough to take the bus myself. It was Mom who found a good teacher in a palace-like children's center converted from a Republican-era Nationalist Party official's residence in the old French concession in Shanghai. Mom would take meticulous notes in class, befriend the other violin-moms, and go shopping the London-Planetree-lined streets after we were done. She watched me practice for an hour every day until I was 15. Mom was always there. Mom was always tough. Mom was always responsible. Mom was always strict. Mom did everything all by herself, cheerfully, with the occasional help from my grandparents. Mom was invincible.

At least it was what she seemed to me. So it was unbelievable to me when she said, "I'm not always like this. I was very naive and dreamy when I was in college," when I resented her for being overly practical and materialistic in high school.

It was also surprising when I found her handwritten romantic quotes on the empty leaves of each and every book she bought over the years. She left encouraging words on the flyleaf of the books she bought for me too, but those are of a different, sentimental tone, a side of her that I had never seen. Most unexpected of all, was how vulnerable and emotional she was in the letters she once wrote to my dad when he was away.

My father did bring home a special gift for my mother: it was the letters she had written to him over the years, and which he had saved. Those letters, in turn, would become an unintended gift for me, because once I learned of their existence, I asked my mother if I could read them. She said I could, but only three; the rest, she said, were too personal. Still, the letters were a window I had never known existed, a window through which I could begin to learn who she was all those years, when he was so far away.

*

She wrote the first letter on the night of May 20, 1993:

"Dear Qin, hope you are well. You are in Lisbon, Portugal now, right? After receiving your letter saying that your return is delayed to August, I have already sent you a short letter. Maybe

you will receive it soon. It's plum rainy season again in a blink of an eye. Now it's pouring outside of my dorm. The pitter-patter raindrop sound complements the music inside the room, accompanying me this whole night till dawn.

"I don't know what's the weather like in Portugal. Is the scenery beautiful? I hope this two, three month of being on land could cultivate your spirit, and improve the depressing, monotonous life.

What I only wish for you, is 'safety,' and then 'health,' and 'happiness.' These three words always resonate in my heart, and I only hope you could hear from afar; I wish you could see my eager heart. Other things are worldly possessions -- you can have them, you can lose them. If you are not safe, if you are not healthy, if you don't have a happy mind, what's left there to talk about?"

"To be honest, I am so worried about you. Because every voyage you take, there's always risks. Besides, the incidents I read about in the newspapers made me worry even more. Fate has tied our lives closely together. I can't help but missing you. So, my dear, please, take care, and take care."

"I'm thinking, on a sunny day when it's nice and peaceful, let's go somewhere together. Because there are many, many beautiful moments in life. What's comforting is that we've been through this couple of years. We still have a lot ahead to face..."

"My dear, please come back to my arms. Please don't leave me again, please let me feel showered by love every minute."

Then she wrote about her job as a teacher, the photos she sent of her trip to Hangzhou, the trips her school organized, and the recent Asian Games: *"The opening ceremony and the closing ceremony were both spectacular, just like what they say on the news. It's perfect. Do you know about it?"*

In the end, my Mom wrote: *"My dear, the food is not good on board, please don't be too strict on yourself. Remember to make a cup of milk every day using the milk powder they distributed. Also, when you get on land, don't be afraid to venture a bit and have a taste of foreign things, since you might not get such a chance again... Just don't disobey the rules. My life is ordinary, nothing special. The only thing that's weighing on me is your return, safely back to my hugs. Kiss you. The family is all good; don't worry. -Jiahua."*

When my Mom wrote this letter, Dad's return from Germany was delayed, because their ship Huada ran into a storm in the Bay of Biscay, and the rudder was damaged. It was a second-hand German ship built in the 1970s and acquired in the 1980s. Dad and his twenty eight crew members spent a worrisome three days floating in the Atlantic Ocean, then they got tugged to the nearest harbor in Portugal. Repairing the ship, finding storage for the thirty thousand tons of chemical fertilizer on board, and acquiring a replacement rudder took some time, so Dad spent an extra three months on land. First in Portugal, then in Spain, and then back in Germany to get the replacement rudder. Dad said he had the best boxed wine, which he had never seen before. He danced with local people in the plaza at night along with other crew members. He had the most fun since starting the voyage and saying bye to Mom a few months before.

In 1993, there were no cell-phones. There was no internet. The only way to connect with and communicate with the land was VHF -- Very High Frequency marine radio. Beyond that, there were only letters. Over the years my parents wrote each other more than eight hundred letters, stuffing two boxes and a few plastic bags stored in the study on the second floor of the suburban house where they now live.

Mom addressed her letter to 20 Guangdong Road, the shipping company Dad was working for at the time, adding -- "transfer to ship 'Huada', Mr. Hu." The company would then deliver the letter to Beijing, where the dispatch services would transfer the letters to the Chinese Embassy in France, which handled all letters to Europe. Sailors enjoyed the privilege of sending their mail as diplomatic letters, which sped their delivery. Still it took a few weeks and even months for Mom's letters to arrive in my Dad's hands. If the ship departed a day after the mailbag arrived, for instance, the letters had to be sent to their next port of call, delaying their arrival. So even though my Mom wrote a letter almost every week, Dad would often hear nothing from home for a month and then receive three or four letters at once. My

Mom told me it was the same with letters from Dad -- he would write regularly without a timely reply.

It was hard for me to picture my Mom writing things like "Come back to my hugs" or "Kiss you." After learning all the trouble my father's ship went through on that voyage, I began to understand. Unlike me, hearing my dad telling the story of that trip, my Mom didn't have the knowledge or means to talk to Dad at the time -- she could only piece things together by waiting for his intermittent letters. Imagine writing a second, then a third letter, only to ask about whether they've received the first. Imagine that everyone around you can actually see and talk to the person they are in love with, and you don't even know where exactly the person you worry so much about is.

*

For centuries, soldiers and sailors have been writing to their families in the way my parents did. The Institute of Historical Research in London did a study on the letters preserved in the National Maritime Museum in London, and made an interesting discovery: the letters sailors and soldiers sent back home were always better preserved than the ones they received. But that was not the case with my Dad, he saved and brought back all the letters my Mom wrote over the years. In fact, he probably got more letters than any of his crewmates. When they reached the harbor, the crew members would rush to get the letters and compete against each other to see who received the most. Dad, along with the senior officer and the third officer, always won. Mom would also enclose self-addressed envelopes. One New Years she sent him a card, along with a long letter. Dad sent the card back, but changed one character so instead of "I love New Year" it read "I love you." Mom wasn't sure if he was too busy to write back, or he meant to appease her fleeting thoughts and urge her to be more realistic and brief.

My parents met in college and before she got married, Mom always felt a sense of being unsettled. This only faded after they had me, which left my Mom little time for

142

emotional thoughts about my Dad. She still missed him, but the content of her letters changed.

As she told me, "I talked about the new prime minister, the stocks, the U.S. dollar currency, and the Asian Games." Mom said that she had to update my Dad with what's going on, otherwise it would be hard for someone to keep up with the society after being isolated in an enclosed environment for so long. "Every time he came back there would be a period of time when he almost seemed like he just got released from a prison, not knowing how to talk to people or act properly in social situations," she said.

When Mom tried to tell me stories from the past, she was calm and articulate as she spoke. Occasionally, she would think of something and it would put a smile on her face. "I had to tell your Dad that his mother was doing well and my job was going well too, so that he wouldn't worry," she said. "He was bad at writing letters but when I complained that he was not romantic enough, he would copy some poems for me. There was one about the sea. It doesn't seem like something your Dad would write."

She also started to write a lot about me. "*It's so heart-wrenching to see her cry after I dropped her off at the kindergarten. If you were here, maybe she wouldn't rely on me so much, but would share some of her love with you, and that would be good.*"

And then, "*I realized that she didn't know the difference between yesterday and the past. At breakfast today we were having porridge, and she said 'Daddy fed me porridge yesterday.' I was so surprised. Because that's weeks ago. It's nice to live like her maybe...*"

When I asked my Mom about these letters she recalled difficult times -- how she got pregnant again when I was two, and had to abort the baby because otherwise she would have lost her job then under China's one-child policy. She also had to move from her in-laws' home in the countryside to Shanghai because I had started school and the schools in the city were considered better. She had to learn how to navigate the local bureaucracy, in time learning how to find a larger, better apartment than the studio we were assigned. My Dad didn't think the studio was so bad, but she insisted I needed my own room and my own desk.

I never felt so different from the other kids growing up, probably because my Mom was so strong, considerate and protective. My Mom wanted to be a writer; she had published a few children's stories. She also tried to start a school for poor children in the city. She taught many Tibetan students, and wanted to teach in the rural mountainous areas of China. But those dreams never fully materialized. She never left the assigned workplace that she was so resolved to leave. "Every morning when I got to that bridge I'd tell myself, 'I'm going to leave this place. One day I am going to leave this place," she said. Tears started streaking down her face and she looked away. "It's been almost thirty years. And I still haven't left that place."

My mother was a middle child and was raised by her grandparents. She always felt that when she became a mother she would give her child the attention she never got from her parents.

*

My father is no longer at sea. He works in an office and is home every night. When he first returned from the sea he didn't know how to use a computer and needed my Mom's help to improve his writing. For a while, before he could find work, we lived on my Mom's salary. My Mom told me that he worried she would leave him, a fate that befalls some men who have spent so many years away at sea.

He needn't have worried. In one of her letters my Mom described an accident when my foot got caught in a bicycle spoke as she was picking me up from school. "*I was scared to death. Of course she cried. I couldn't sleep all night. The next morning they said the bone was not broken but it would take at least a week to heal. The first three day I would hold her or she would lay in bed. Then I carried her on my back.*"

My Mom somehow thought the accident was her fault, and wondered how she might have prevented it. She wanted him to know I was okay and that she was, too.

Still, she added, "*If you were home maybe this kind of accident wouldn't have happened.*"

15.

Paris Broke Us Both
Leena Sanzgiri

By the time I met Mr. Negandhi, the family home had been crumbling for years. My parents and I were seated in his office as his assistant pulled out enormous files. Mr. Negandhi was in his eighties and had been representing the Sanzgiris for two generations. We were finalizing the sale of Shiv Kunj, meaning the House of Shiva. Once a luxurious Mumbai bungalow, it was now only regularly inhabited by ageing servants, monsoon rats, and the ghosts of the Sanzgiris who died there prematurely.

Mr. Negandhi looked about as decrepit as the house had become, but he was still a sharp lawyer. I'd heard lore of his wit and sarcasm. Upon introduction, he immediately asked me, "Are you married?"

"No," I replied, irritated.

He snorted. "This one won't get married. There's always a Sanzgiri woman who doesn't."

My mother gave a defensive retort I can't recall; my father, oblivious, remained absorbed in paperwork; and my mind drifted to the woman who had recently lived out Negandhi's prophecy. Nayana.

She was my father's sister, a favorite aunt who had died five years earlier, in 2003. We had much in common, from unmanageable curly hair and scrawny limbs as children, to a love of languages and bawdy humor as adults. But at the core of our bond was Paris, because it broke us both.

When Paris broke me, it was violent, a harrowing blur that left me curled up and alone on a sidewalk, when Nayana was already gone. But Paris broke her in a different way, insidiously becoming the metaphor for so many things in her life that were not meant to be.

*

Nayana Mangesh Sanzgiri was born on July 4, 1954 in

the affluent neighborhood of Girgaon in Mumbai. She was the youngest of four siblings in a well-to-do Maharashtran family: two sisters, ten-year-old Meena and four-year-old Jyotsna; and my father Sunil, the lone Sanzgiri son born squarely between them. My grandfather, Mangesh, was forty then, my grandmother, Suhasini, a year his junior. Mangesh's younger sister, Manorama, never married and lived with the family all through her long life, referred to by all as "Atya," the specific Marathi term for father's sister.

Mangesh was a lawyer who earned a comfortable living, but whose sprawling properties in the heart of Mumbai were the rewards of previous generations of family wealth. Summers were spent in a vacation home in Lonavala, a lush hill station in the Western Ghats of Maharashtra. A falling out with his brother led to jagged splits in the family fortune over the course of the years to come, and even though Nayana was a welcome addition to this branch of the Sanzgiris, she arrived at a time when the family had started to shrink.

Nayana was born with a twin. That is what her best friend, Ameeta, told me one day, without fanfare, but simply to make the point: "She wasn't a very healthy child. They were twins, and her parents lost the other."

Ameeta went on -- not anticipating my shocked response of actually dropping the phone -- to say that Nayana wasn't sure when her twin died. "Maybe the older kids would know," she said. But my father and aunt had no recollection of any twin. Perhaps the twin died in the womb. Still, the loss of the twin -- real, or imagined -- defined something of Nayana's young life: illness and the loss of a lifelong partner.

Shiv Kunj was located in Juhu, far from the central, trendier neighborhoods where the family had lived. The transition was harder on her parents and Jyotsna, but Nayana was too young to notice, and Shiv Kunj was seductively impressive, a standalone bungalow in one of the most densely packed cities in the world. After Jyotsna left for college, Nayana was the only child living in Shiv Kunj. She had no inkling of how prolonged and curtailed that status would be.

*

At the age of fifteen, at Elphinstone College in Mumbai, Nayana and Ameeta met for the first time. It wasn't a quick friendship for that age; they gravitated towards each other in a steady and natural way. They were compatible in that they complemented each other, though they were not outwardly alike. Ameeta was far more serious with an appreciation for humor, while Nayana was a card, but prone to moodiness. The two girls also found an unforeseen need in one another, a mutual trust that would let them start to break free of their families.

Together, alongside a few other girlfriends in school, they began to enjoy the quiet thrills of mild adolescent rebellion. They weren't a wild bunch, but they would occasionally meet up with boys without their parents' knowledge. One Holi, a spring festival in which crowds throw bright, powdered colors at each other outside, eight friends piled into a car and snuck off to Juhu Beach, not far from Shiv Kunj. Among them was a handsome young man named Jagdish, slightly older than Nayana, who was taken by her wit and her boldness. Within the week, he had written a poem for Nayana about that day on the beach, a clumsy set of verses about the sun and the sand. He invited Nayana to coffee with a few other friends, and although she did go, she rebuffed his advances, knowing that her parents wouldn't approve. She was too young to be married, and "dating" was not an acceptable concept.

It was Nayana's first brush with romance, and she found confidence in refusing her suitor. She was coming out of her shell, and by the time she was twenty, she had left Shiv Kunj and Mumbai, and she was studying at Jawaharlal Nehru University in Delhi. She had declared herself a French major, focusing on language rather than literature, with thoughts that she would one day teach as a French professor. But there was a much more pressing goal she had in mind -- her dream was to complete a *maitrise* at the Sorbonne, as she had seen a handful of her classmates before her do. She applied for a scholarship through the agency of the French government that awarded scholarships to foreign students.

To her delight, she was one of fewer than ten students in India to be awarded a two-year scholarship to attend the Sorbonne Nouvelle that year. By then, all of Nayana's siblings were abroad; Meena was in Manila, and Jyotsna and my father were both in the U.S. Although her parents worried about her leaving for a country whose native tongue was foreign to them, they agreed that she should go. My grandparents were progressively proud of the ambitions of their daughters, well ahead of their time. They were not preoccupied with arranging a marriage for Nayana, who was twenty four when she set off for her life's greatest adventure. In 1978, she headed to Paris.

*

Two terrorist incidents bookended Nayana's time in Paris. Just a few months before she arrived in 1978, three Palestinians opened fire on Orly airport. In 1980, soon after she left, a Parisian synagogue was bombed. Both tragedies were, of course, unrelated to her life, other than that they were symbolic markers for how her time in Paris would have such a definitive start and end, and how it would not be the idyll she had envisioned.

When I asked Jyotsna about Nayana's time in Paris, her response jarred me. "Paris broke her heart," she said sadly, even though she admitted she knew very little of Nayana's time there. In fact, all of Nayana's living family knew next to nothing about her Paris years, even though she was very much defined and lauded for having studied there. Jyotsna said that pervasive racism in the city got to Nayana over time. Ameeta, on the other hand, attributed Nayana's heartache to a romance that went sour. Abha Chatterjee, one of Nayana's classmates in Paris, remembers things differently.

Nayana and Abha stayed at the Cité Universitaire, where I myself would stay as a student nearly thirty years later. Both women opted against staying in the Maison de l'Inde, the Indian dorm; they had come to France to meet students from other cultures, to experience all they could that was new. Nayana lived in the Brazilian dorm, while

Abha lived in the Mexican dorm.

One of Nayana's first friends was a man named Raimundo, who, as Abha put it, was "gay at a time when it was really hard to be gay." Raimundo would make them Brazilian food, and they would all linger over meals in the university cafeteria. Halfway into Nayana's first year in Paris, she, Abha, and another friend, Ramnath Narayanswamy, began to share all of the responsibilities of their meals, taking turns doing the shopping, the cooking, and the cleaning up. Ramnath was a Marxist in the classic ways of a graduate student; his Marxism swelled and spouted out of him with the whiskey he would drink after dinner. Nayana and Abha sipped on wine and debated with him, sometimes just to poke fun at him, other times with more fervor.

Abha was a member at the cinema club at the Centre Georges Pompidou, and Nayana grew to love Kurosawa films, as well as French and American movies and music. That Christmas, another friend, Shobana, was marrying a Frenchman against her parents' wishes, so Nayana, Abha, and Ramnath represented the bride's family, making sandwiches that morning for the simple reception that evening. Nayana's world was expanding, and with it, a new-found confidence of adulthood and trust in her future.

Abha does not recall experiencing the cultural shock of overt racism, saying instead that it was really the North African students who bore the bigger brunt of the prejudice of Paris. But there was one cultural norm that was out of the ordinary -- for the first time, they were all free to date without worrying about their families' approval. She knows that Nayana grew close to an Algerian friend, but Nayana never talked explicitly with Abha about having a boyfriend. Nayana was private, choosy about whom she confided in, and Ameeta only learned about this relationship after Nayana had returned to India from Paris. Even then, Nayana was tight-lipped on the subject, saying that he had broken things off, and she accepted it and moved on as best she could.

That break-up happened as Nayana was transitioning from her first year in Paris to her second, which would shift

her experience seismically. Abha was a year ahead of
Nayana, ready to go back to India, when Nayana got the
abrupt news that her scholarship would not be continued
during her second year in France. Although Nayana was
doing well in her classes, relations between India and
Western countries had become strained because of India's
expanding nuclear program, and the French government cut
off her award for the second year.

Nayana had to very suddenly make ends meet for all of
her expenses. She started to work as an au pair and
babysitter, and this is where Jyotsna said Nayana
experienced racism first-hand, in the homes of others. She
took odd jobs and rattled away on her manual typewriter
late into the night, trying to finish her thesis as soon as
possible. Whatever hopes she had of extending her visa and
staying on in Paris were dashed. Around this time, she sent
a distressed letter to her older sisters, not mentioning any
romantic heartbreak, but professing her frustration with the
city she so wanted to call home.

Her siblings were concerned, and they discussed going
to visit Nayana to comfort her. But by then, Meena had two
young children in the Philippines, and Jyotsna was in
California. They had left home when Nayana was young,
and they didn't know Nayana the woman very well. They
both opted not to visit Nayana, a decision Jyotsna still
regrets.

So Nayana prepared to return to Shiv Kunj. She was
grateful, after that year in flux, to be taken care of again in
her family home. And she was flush with youthful optimism
that she would surely return to Paris to live, that she would
have another chance to make it her own.

*

In 1981, about six months after Nayana returned to
Mumbai, my parents repatriated from the U.S. back to India,
and moved in to Shiv Kunj with their son and daughter,
Sunkait and Seema. Shiv Kunj was in its bustling heyday;
the prodigal son had come home from America, Mangesh
and Suhasini were aging but in manageably good health,

Atya was a loving, doting presence, and four servants attended to everyone's needs.

Nayana had recently been hired into the position she would hold for the rest of her life, teaching French at Sophia College. Her boss, Pervine Bhujwala, remembers Nayana's interview clearly. She was waiting with my grandfather outside of the principal's office, skinny like a teenager, but sharply dressed in an impeccably pressed sari. She was eloquent and had excellent command of the language -- "better than I did," Pervine acknowledged -- and she was offered a job a few days later.

It was an exciting time for Nayana; she loved her new job, even though it was nearly a two-hour commute from Shiv Kunj. She had fallen back into step easily with Ameeta and her group of friends and made new ones at Sophia. With the arrival of my parents, she did not have to bear the sole responsibility of caring for the older generation. She found welcome friendship in her brother and sister-in-law, and adored her nephew and niece. And she was ready to think about marriage.

While her parents would have accepted a suitable love marriage, Nayana had not met anyone on her own, and she was ready to meet potential suitors via arranged marriage. But it wasn't easy -- she was twenty-seven, and older than most women of the time looking to get married. And as Ameeta put it bluntly, "We both had a hard time finding an arranged match. I was too dark for families' liking, and Nayana was not that good-looking."

It is true that Nayana was not the most attractive woman, but she was educated, had a steady job, and was from an esteemed family in a beautiful home. But when it came to marriage, Shiv Kunj would get in her way. She was introduced to a man named Sanjiv Kohli, a distant family friend who seemed to take to her. The two were eventually engaged. At a gathering in Shiv Kunj to celebrate the betrothed couple, Sanjiv got belligerently drunk, and was eventually put into a rickshaw and sent home by my angry father.

As things began to unravel, it became clear that Sanjiv was more interested in inheriting Shiv Kunj than he was in

Nayana. He insisted that they start their new life in the family home; moving into the bride's ancestral home after marriage was practically unheard of in India then. Nayana was much more keen on starting a new life with her husband-to-be, outside of Shiv Kunj. She had no notion whatsoever that Shiv Kunj was hers for the taking. Her mother often likened her to Yudhishtira, the character from the Mahabharata epic, whose fairness was often the cause of his undoing. Nayana and the family realized that Sanjiv was more interested in the property than in his fiancée. Jyotsna even recalls a rumor that he had another serious relationship in another town. The engagement broke off within a few months.

My father and Nayana met with a few other potential grooms, but nothing came of it. Pervine remembers her arriving at work regaling them with stories of men who claimed to be in their thirties and successful, and were in reality at least a decade older and unemployed (not unlike modern workplace gossip of tales of online dating). Shiv Kunj put stars in the eyes of those willing to marry an older (read: not yet thirty), plain woman, but her independence, education, and fierce protection of her family kept her from falling for them.

Jyotsna says that Nayana grew out of wanting to get married from these disappointments, but my mother contradicts this flatly. "Every time we gave her a gift, for the rest of her life, it was a running joke that it was meant for her trousseau," she says. "I remember that so clearly. She laughed about it, but it was something she always wanted." Ameeta and Abha agree.

*

In 1982, the tides began to turn in Shiv Kunj. Sunkait, my older brother, was starting to show some changes after his tenth birthday. His eye was drooping, his speech was slightly slurred, and drool would occasionally collect at the corners of his mouth. After having a seizure at home, he was rushed to the hospital, where a neurologist confirmed the unthinkable. Sunkait, Shiv Kunj's son's son, had a brain tumor and was unlikely to survive.

The next year passed in a blur of surgeries, chemotherapy, radiation, trips to and from the U.S., increasingly desperate efforts to save Sunkait's life. Nayana was the point person on the ground, rushing to and from the hospital to help my parents, to watch after my sister Seema, and to provide as much emotional support as she could. But no one could safeguard Sunkait from the treachery of his cancer. On September 14, 1983, as my father wrote later in a memoir:

"The weeping women were herded out the room, and my son drifted into yesterday."

Sunkait's loss reverberated throughout the halls of the house. In some sense, my mother says the older generation took it the hardest, because they were so confounded at outliving their grandchild. My father, being the more emotional of my two parents and a prolific writer, wrote on what would have been Sunkait's fortieth birthday, "Burden? Why the hell do we need to carry a burden like this? And who has retribution's key? God bless you, my son, I sincerely hope you found an everlasting peace. I surely did not."

My mother was stoic, the rock who held things together for Seema. But both parents agreed -- they could no longer stay in the home where their son had died. Nayana too was devastated by the loss of her nephew, and she was distressed that my parents were moving back to America. But there was a bit of news that had her equally disturbed -- my mother was pregnant with me, about ten months after Sunkait's passing.

Ameeta told me that Nayana was angry with my parents, that she thought they were trying to replace the child they lost too quickly. My thoughts spun wildly at this revelation; this aunt I had so loved had initially spurned my conception. But I was appreciative for this truth. It was one of the first times anyone had spoken to me with real honesty about Nayana, without weaving her into spinster sainthood. It was when she came into focus for me as a real and complex woman, an objectively good person who harbored human unpleasantness she had every right to.

My parents and Seema left for America in 1985, and

Nayana was again the only one of her generation living with her parents and Atya. A few years later, Ameeta would get married. Nayana became extremely close to Ameeta's husband, Dharam -- they were similar in their boldness, humor, and honesty. The couple were Nayana's closest friends for the remainder of her life. But Ameeta had moved into a new chapter, of marriage and then motherhood, the paths to which Nayana could not find the way.

*

In my childhood, Nayana was a benign and welcome presence, a young and boisterous aunt who would visit every few years, bringing exotic presents and a Toblerone from a London airport into my American life. When we visited India, Nayana and her friends were a fun and motley crew, filling Shiv Kunj with celebration and life. She was a beloved professor, the kind who was very tough on her students but who would also spearhead a faculty parody of Backstreet Boys songs for school-wide talent shows.

As I grew more interested in French in high school, Nayana became a fixture of my fascination. I wondered at her time in Paris, marveling at her sense of adventure and love of the language. Yet the shyness and selfishness of adolescence precluded me from asking her much about it.

In the photo that inspired this story taken by my father, Nayana, my mother, and I are standing in front of the Eiffel Tower. Each of us has degrees of joy on their faces -- my mother's is unbridled, mine is mixed with the self-consciousness of a teenager, and Nayana's is far from apparent. She, if anyone, looks the most serious and out of place.

But she was our expert tour guide, whipping us through the city with ease and never stumbling over the language. Shortly after this photo was taken, as we sat down to lunch on the Champ de Mars, my mother prodded me to speak to Nayana in French. I glared at my mother; I was far from ready to speak to a French professor, and I was nervous to do so with a relative. Nayana kept her face mostly blank, but I could sense her looking at me quizzically. I excused myself and stomped to the bathroom. I returned, slightly mollified, and said tentatively to Nayana, "Ça va?" We exchanged about three sentences, and that was the extent of our French conversation during the eighteen years our lives overlapped. She would not be around to see me live in the Cité Universitaire in 2006 as she had done decades before. For that day, she could only express a small bit of pride that I was showing interest in her field.

Later that afternoon, my father's wallet was stolen in the Metro, and Nayana became the police intermediary. Instead of a peaceful sojourn, Nayana spent most of the four-day trip at the most touristy destinations, translating for the chambermaid, and filing police reports. We did not once go to anywhere she had lived or loved or loathed. I wonder if she was reliving all that Paris did and was to her, how it set into motion the events that would send and keep her in Shiv Kunj, if she was increasingly angry at being tethered to her family yet again in the only city where she had been truly free.

My parents returned to Paris six years after that trip, when I was spending the summer alone in Paris, researching my undergraduate senior thesis. I had spent a good portion of my junior year abroad in Paris alongside my classmates, but this was a real solo venture; I knew no one save for a few French friends I had made in previous semesters. It was 2006, the 5th of July, a day after Nayana's and America's birthdays. France had just defeated Portugal in a world-cup semi-final, and as my thesis advisor would put it later, "Those wins make for fascist mobs." Crowds were going wild throughout Paris, and I returned back to the dorm late and alone.

I entered the iron gates, and it happened so swiftly I couldn't scream. He held my neck against the grill and dropped my pants, and it took a few moments before I knew searing pain. He thrust me back against the gate and removed himself from me, and only when I saw the flash of his penis did I realize what had happened. As he ran away, he hollered, "Je ne t'ai pas fait amour," which literally means, "I didn't make love to you," and generally means, "I didn't have sex with you," and based on what the police thought, may have meant, "I didn't ejaculate in you." What I did know was that I had been raped by a stranger in a city I loved, and like Nayana, so wanted to make my own.

My sister flew in a few days later with her new husband, and I told only them. My parents arrived a week later not because they knew what happened, but because we had already planned a family trip to coincide with my time in Paris. I refused to tell them of my rape; it was the one thing I could do to protect the people who had effectively protected me from harm my entire life. Instead, I did as Nayana had done. I proved an efficient and impressive tour guide, I let them set the itinerary of what we were to do, and I let any of the traces of how I was broken dissipate in the objective beauty of Paris.

And I thought of her the entire time, because I'm quite sure that's how she did it.

*

About six months after Nayana took my parents and me through Paris, she was diagnosed with stage IV ovarian cancer. She had been complaining of her feet swelling, and some bleeding, but otherwise had not talked of any major health concerns. The reality was that as an unmarried woman in the early 2000s in Mumbai, she would have never been seen by a gynecologist, and if she was, she would not have been administered a Pap smear. The assumption was that a single woman would have to be a virgin, so what was the need for such testing? It was another slap in the face by the disappointment of not getting married, and in so many things that had left her unfulfilled.

The previous years had been hard on Nayana. Her mother had suffered two strokes and was bedridden, unable to speak. Atya had trouble walking, with such stiff joints that her knees could no longer bend. Shiv Kunj was getting harder to maintain; the flamboyantly painted walls, once invitingly cheerful, now had films of dust on them. Cracks were appearing in the floors, and many of its rooms remained vacant. Nayana was the only person who went upstairs, and fewer and fewer people came every year for the annual Ganesh Chathurthi holiday, a major religious festival that once drew dozens of people to Shiv Kunj in its prime. Abha remembers visiting Nayana just before she got sick. Nayana walked in with armloads of vegetables and the stress of her two-hour commute still written on her face.

Nayana fought her cancer hard, and with characteristic humor. But the toxicity of chemotherapy would turn her skin an inhumanly reddish-gray, as she would pace the room with nausea and stinging sensations throughout her body. My mother was her main caretaker in the family, flying in as often as possible to nurse another cancer sufferer in Shiv Kunj. Ameeta, Dharam, and Nayana's friends took turns providing her care in Shiv Kunj, then eventually in the hospital, then eventually keeping vigil as she was intubated, my father holding her hand. In the weeks leading up to her death, Nayana worried constantly about her mother and Atya, issuing instructions for their care after she was gone, divulging the codes for safes, and the locations of keys to all the closets in the house. But that last day in the hospital, she was done. She asked to be taken off life support, and after several hours of labored breathing, she closed her eyes. She was free.

I was told about Nayana's passing by our cook, who said in her broken English, "Nayana Atya is no more." My mother was already out preparing funeral arrangements, my father was in Shiv Kunj. I sat in silence, and I blinked. It was not until much later that I cried.

Mr. Negandhi would inextricably link Nayana and me five years later, after I myself had lived through gut-wrenching happiness and pain in Paris. Atya, the Sanzgiri sister of her generation who never married, was the last to die in Shiv Kunj, and it was time to sell the property. Nayana's dream had been to tear it down and build an apartment building, with flats for all of the siblings.

Shiv Kunj was sold to a Gujarati businessman who had similar hopes, and who tore down the house, but has struggled to complete a replacement. When I was last in Mumbai we happened to drive by where Shiv Kunj had stood. There was a concrete structure still being built but it was impossible to tell what it would one day look like, or be.

Though I missed the house, I found myself wishing that its replacement would have by then been completed. With so much history, so much horrible history, I was hoping that whoever came to live there would do so without the pain and the loss of Shiv Kunj.

The last time I was there, Nayana was in intensive care, dying. I went to visit her and when I left, I knew I would never see her again. In the years since, I have grown closer to her than I was when she was alive, because I was able to see Nayana the woman, Nayana the Parisian, as I myself grew into both identities.

But Mr. Negandhi could not know how much his prediction would upset me for years afterward. I am single. I have dealt with illness. I have been broken by Paris. But does that make me fated to be like Nayana? Shiv Kunj is gone. Perhaps with it, a spell has been broken. I do not know what the house will look like.

16.

It's Not About the Boy
Heather Schröering

His name is Rip. I know that because, well, it's none of my business. Why someone took a picture of this boy in a button-down shirt on a battleship is none of my business -- nor is anything he did on that vacation with his family in 1972.

Yet those memories live on my bookcase -- discarded snapshots of them at least. It's none of my business how Rip's family photo album ended up there, by way of an antique shop in southern Illinois. But collecting old photos is my business. And when people leave their stuff around for someone else to claim, well perhaps we shouldn't lose things if we don't want to be found.

That's where this story begins, with a thrift store find. But not mine exactly. Like they say about great adventures finding you, people with a strange love of collecting dead people's stuff find each other. That's how Rip's photo album ended up with me, but my friend Madeline Northway had it first.

She was expecting little more than bad coffee and a bathroom break, when she made a stop at the antique mall, one of a few favorites dotting Route 66 last summer. The shop was junkier than it was when she was a little girl, when she wandered through Illinois' resale stores with her mother, looking for treasures to take home to her own shop in St. Louis.

Now the store is more of a nostalgic halfway point for Madeline, on her drives back home from Chicago, where she's a fashion photographer. Outside, bird baths, a rusty wagon wheel, and chain-link gates for sale lined the long A-frame sheet-metal building that nearly stands alone on the flat stretch of road off I-55. Inside was like window shopping dozens of mini-stores, with rows and rows of booths filled with milk glass vases, beat-up auto signs, a full-sized taxidermied bear going for $1,250.

Somewhere between the still-full limited-edition Coca-Cola bottles and enamel-coated teapots, Madeline unearthed an unusually large book bound in cherry-red tweed fabric. In the right-hand corner of the cover was a silvery plate that read, "ALBUM."

Paging through the photos, their cellophane coverings crunching beneath her fingers, she saw women dancing in mint-green bell-bottom suits, teenage boys in paisley button-down shirts, and holiday gatherings with bouffanted ladies smoking cigarettes around dining room tables. The clothes, the houses, the interiors with "swag globe lights" -- she had to have the photo album. For $5, it was hers.

Madeline texted me photos of the album. Where she saw a historical representation of fashion, I saw nuances of vacationing in the 1970s. Where she saw design inspiration for her next photo shoot, I saw beaches and boardwalks I wanted to locate. Where she saw new home decor, I saw a little boy on a ship who's likely a man now missing his family photo album.

I had to find him.

My treasure hunt began when I received the album from Madeline in the mail on a Friday night. I flipped through the pages of instant film snapshots, gasping slightly each time I laid eyes on the few glossy rectangular prints taken on a Polaroid Land Camera, a coveted film that's discontinued.

And then I saw him, the boy looking through the round door of a ship. On the white border of the Kodak Instamatic print is a date stamped in blue, May 1972. I folded back the cellophane and peeled the photo from the page, revealing blue-inked scribbling. The wiry cursive read "battleship Ala."

Had I just seen the writing by itself -- as I had first seen the photo in Madeline's text -- I would have called up my browser, dying to pin down the location as soon as possible. But I was captivated by the album spread of other pictures from the road same trip, with secrets no internet search engine could impart. With every photo, another clue.

The brown-haired boy riding a droopy-faced horse statue in front of a wooden building with a sign that says "Wells Fargo Stage." "6 gun," the loopy handwritten letters on the back told me. The boy, not even ten years old, sitting atop a stationary covered wagon next to a man in sunglasses who's huddled in the photo prop clearly meant for children. The back read "6 gun territory."

And then, on the back of a wide shot of the boy and the man standing by an enormous propeller, was the second clue: "Rip and I in front of prop. of battleship."

Rip. This must the boy.

I'd learned as much as I could from that spread and moved on to others where I saw Rip wearing red swim trunks on a white sand beach or standing under a Palm Pavilion sign selling snacks and Solarcaine. After such success, I was sure the snapshots wanted me to know more.

I peeled dozens and dozens of delicate photos from the album pages, yellowed from decades-old glue. The Kodaks came right off, but the Polaroid Land film was less agreeable and began to tear at the pages. I left those alone.

But the more I peeled, the less I learned. Few of the remaining photos had captions, and those that did weren't very useful.

"Taken Easter before going to church."

"This dress...doesn't look too bad. I've had it since 1967 just couldn't give away."

"Pigs in water."

By the time I finished all I knew was that a boy named Rip visited "battleship Ala." once in May 1972 and in the same month took a picture with a man named Joe, who may or may not be his grandfather.

I revisited each of the labeled photos, flipping them over again and again, as if begging the cursive letters to reveal something else to me that wasn't there the last time. Nothing inspired me. So I went for the finicky Polaroids, certain were hiding something.

And I was right. The answer was behind a photo of two women posing in a backyard garden on a sunny day. I recognized the one of the right, a white-haired lady in purple slacks. I pulled at the corner of the picture. There on the back between the glue stains was an address.

I flipped through the album, searching for where else I had seen the white-haired woman squinting in the sun. I stopped on a page with two side-by-side snapshots of Rip and others standing on a lawn under a white scalloped awning protruding from a mobile home. In both photos, the same house number written on the Polaroid.

I plugged the address into my browser. The first result took me to a photo of a freshly paved street lined with palm trees and tiny white mobile homes with tiny manicured lawns--just like the ones in the album.

When I tried the address in a public records database to find the owners, the couple on the deed were Joe and Mary with an Italian last name. But my searches for Rip with that surname failed. I had to turn back to the photos.

I began to build a family tree. Mary, the woman with white curls, and Joe, a tan man with dark slicked-back hair, are Rip's grandparents. They're stars of the album, a window into their retirement life of sunshine and short sleeves in December. Their world is captured in snapshots of friends and family who maybe love to spend a lot of time with Mary and Joe, or maybe love that they have a vacation home someplace warm.

And that home -- where the palm leaf wallpaper clashes with the Christmas tree in the sunroom, but the pineapple upside-down cake is good for any occasion -- is straight from the set of a '70s film called "American Dream: Florida Vacation." (Brown station wagon topped with luggage rack under the carport included.)

Between photos of nameless people in bathing suits and school pictures of towheaded children, Rip and his family float in and out of the frames for special occasions and summers. In the winter, he opens gifts with his older brother and sister. In spring, he sits in front of a birthday cake with his name on it that Mary holds up for the picture, her signature pose for these events.

There are a lot of these birthday photos, with round cakes addressed to its recipient so everyone knows whose lucky day it is. But the only names I could make out were those I already knew -- Rip and Joe. One particular photo shows Rip's dad with his arm around a proud-looking Grandma Mary, his mother, who's posing with an elaborate confection decorated with a pink polka-dotted bikini.

I kept returning to this photo, demanding it to tell me the name scrawled in frosted letters between the flaming candles protruding out of the busty headless cake lady. "Happy Birthday Sp---." I couldn't make it out. I began to wonder if I had it all wrong. Is Grandma Mary even Rip's grandma? What in the hell kind of name is Rip anyway?

I was at a dead end and needed a break from the album. I felt like I was in one of those conversations with a friend, who starts a sentence with something gripping and refuses to tell you the rest because they've said too much. I went back to my browser to see what I could find about Joe and Mary.

I hunted for anyone with the surname. I found a young sitcom actor, a Greek countess who married an Italian nobleman, and a murdered St. Louis mobster who was linked to a slot-machine war in the 1930s. But after hours of searching, no sign of Rip.

*

I don't try to track down people in all the old photos I collect. In fact, I've never done this before. The first picture of a stranger I ever bought was from an estate sale in Kentucky. It's a posed portrait of a woman clutching a swathe of her floral dress. She's looking over her shoulder, smiling with her eyes. I needed this picture. I'm not sure why. But after I bought it, a message inked in the bottom corner of the photo resonated with me.

The handwritten letters: "Lest you forget. With love, Sarah."

The more I looked at it, the more it stirred a sadness in me. Her note, in one way or another, got separated from whomever it was for. Despite her wishes, it became this forgotten object in a for-sale box. But it was mine now, and I felt responsible for giving it a second life. I found more Sarahs at the next estate sale and soon enough became the keeper of a trove of strangers in black and white, hoarding their orphan memories like my own.

But Rip wasn't like the Sarahs. These weren't hundred-year-old portraits of people who are long dead and gone. I had to keep looking.

The final clue was in an obituary. Not Rip's thankfully. It was his father, Kenneth "Spud," the "Sp" name I couldn't make out on the cake.

I had found the boy on the ship.

*

Days after my hunt for Rip, in an antique store in small-town east Texas, I rummaged through boxes and boxes of discarded memories -- loose photos from the '20s and '30s, posed portraits of girls in frilly dresses, shirtless men working in fields.

At the cash register, as a dealer rang up some black-and-white pictures I picked out of a couple at the beach in the '40s, I wondered aloud: How do people lose track of this stuff? She shrugged and told me she sells old portraits of her own family members at her booth.

"I don't have any idea who they are," she said through a taffy-like drawl. "Somebody else might want 'em."

Weirdos like me want them. But if buying them makes me a little weird, it's not nearly as weird as the red album for sale at the antique mall in the first place. Madeline, my partner-in-weird who encourages this strange obsession, agrees.

"Every time my dad comes across an old photo, all seven of his brothers and sisters demand a copy," she said on the phone to me one day. "Coming across an entire album, the chances of it getting lost and ending up in an antique mall are pretty slim, when where there's so many different people, who would be interested in preserving these memories."

I couldn't know if I didn't reach out to Rip. The public records search I used to find him told me that his current phone number was unlisted but did offer a handful of old numbers.

I dialed the first number. Putting the phone to my ear, a wave of nervousness washed over me, a Pavlovian condition, despite my eight years of reporting and cold calling strangers. But the line was dead. All that build-up for nothing. I tried the second one, which went to the voicemail of a much older-sounding man that couldn't possibly be Rip. The third try was a repeat of my first, which left me with only one more number.

I typed it into my phone and at the first low-pitched ring--the sound of a strand of tiny bubbles forcing their way through my speaker--I had a feeling it wouldn't be long until Rip was on the other end of the line. It rang a second time. Then a third. And a fourth. And then I lost count.

But I persisted. I was going to stay on that call until someone answered or my phone died. And then someone answered, a familiar voice.

"We're sorry," a woman's tone came through the phone. "You have reached a number that has been disconnected or is no longer in service."

Until that moment, I hadn't realized how nasally that robotic voice was, nor had I been so disappointed to hear it. Surely, Rip will be happy to hear from me and to know his family heirloom has been rescued from all those odd birds who collect other people's stuff. And let's not even talk about the crusties who sell that stuff for money.

My last resort was to send a message to Rip's Facebook inbox, which is where messages from strangers go to die. I had nothing left to do but wait to never hear from Rip.

But only a few days later, I had a missed call from an area code I didn't recognize. Confident it was Rip, I called back.

When I began this treasure hunt, I dreamed up what I thought my conversation with Rip might go like. I thought this would be a moment when two strangers connect over this incredibly odd situation that just happened to bring them together. I thought this red photo album got separated from this family, and, like when someone returns your wallet with the hundred-dollar bill you had in there intact, he'd tell me he thought those pictures were gone forever.

That's not how this conversation went.

Rip answered when I called back, and everything I had prepared to say left my brain. And in my excitement hearing from him, I blurted out, "I just got really obsessed with finding you and wanted to return this photo album."

There was silence. I told him it was rare to find photos of people who might still be alive. That probably didn't help. More silence.

I asked, "Do you want it back."

To which he replied, "Yeah, I'll call you tomorrow. I'm with my son right now."

I assume he had to wash all of his shoe laces and sort his socks the next day because he never called.

"He probably thought you were such a weirdo," Madeline said to me on the phone. "He probably thought you were a stalker."

"Probably," I said

"I think that creeped him out," she laughed. I guess she thought I didn't hear "weirdo" and "stalker" the first time.

"Yeah that word," I said. "I usually would never have used that word."

"Oh my gosh, you totally creeped him out."

But I guess I am a little obsessed. In the way psychiatrists draw associations between intrusive thoughts? No. Although Rip probably thinks I'm unwell. But in terms of dwelling on how sad it is that a stranger ended up with snapshots of a family's past? Yes.

I'm haunted by the idea of being separated from memories that can never be retrieved. And the possibility that such a personal item could be intentionally discarded, I can't accept that. My fascination with old photos is directly connected to this fear I have of forgetting, aware that memory is already a tenuous mechanism.

*

There wasn't much left behind when my grandmother died. It wasn't because she never had anything. She was a giver, which translates to easy prey in the language of takers.

"I remember coming through the house after she died and feeling like so many people had already taken stuff," my cousin Melody told me. "I kept thinking, I don't care if I have anything of hers because I have my memories. That's what I kept telling myself."

I was fifteen, and what I did have from her was seemingly endless documentation of our family in pictures. In my favorite, she's wearing a bathing suit, assuming a power stance with her hands on her hips, lips pursed. This is how I remembered her. Full of life, an unwavering female force -- five-foot-three and entirely terrifying yet feeling no terror.

Smiling was usually only caught in candid moments, with her head leaning back mid-laugh.

"When I see her in those pictures with her mouth open laughing," Melody said, "it just takes me back to that moment when she was making you feel like you were the best person in the world."

I studied them, obsessing over the nuances of my grandmother's features. I paid special attention to her hands, such an easy thing to forget. I just never wanted to look down at my own hands and wonder where they came from.

"Every time I see a picture of her -- because there are so few of those -- I think 'God I wish I could have had more,'" Melody said. "You don't think about that stuff until it's too late."

That's the thing about hindsight and perhaps the tangibility of photos. There's comfort in knowing they exist. They're heirlooms to be cherished and guarded. They're there when memory fails you. But these photos aren't just preserved memories. They are reminders of what and who used to be. Of what you can't get back.

So, Rip, if you're reading this, you're welcome to have your photo album back.

But for now, his seven-year-old self will remain on my bookshelf, next to the other discarded strangers' snapshots. It's none of my business how his family photo album ended up in an antique shop. Because it's not about the boy.

About the Authors

Jordan Nadler is a New York City-based writer and editor who has a thing for Anais Nin and Zelda Fitgerald. Find her on Twitter @Nadleresque and Instagram @nadleresque.

Linh Nguyen is a New York-based journalist from Ho Chi Minh City, Vietnam who loves anything written by Natsuo Kirino and Ruth Ware. Connect with her on Twitter and LinkedIn @linhbnguyen or at linhpnguyen018@gmail.com.

Chloe Picchio is a New York-based writer and photographer who loves anything by Margaret Atwood. Connect with her on Twitter @ChloePicchio or Instagram @chloecaldwell.

Deanna Hirsch is a Denver based writer who loves anything by Nora Ephron. Connect with her on Twitter @DeannaHirsch or email deahirs@gmail.com.

Zein Jardaneh is a Jordanian writer based in New York who loves anything by Hisham Matar and Thrity Umrigra. Connect with her on Twitter @zeinbjardaneh or at zein.jardaneh@gmail.com.

Will McCollister is a New York-based writer from Ironton, Ohio and his favorite authors are J.R.R. Tolkien and Mark Twain. Follow him on Twitter: @WillMcCollister or Instagram: @william_mccollister.

Reh Blazier is an Arizona native who still won't declare a New York residency, a podcast enthusiast, and will read anything by Haruki Murakami. Connect with her on Twitter @KelsieBlazier or email kelsieblazier@gmail.com.

Sage Kendahl Howard is a Brooklyn-based writer who loves anything by Octavia Butler. Connect with her on Instagram @sagekendahl or email sage.howard916@gmail.com.

J.W. Kash is a New York City-based writer who likes to read Thomas Wolfe, Emily Brontë, and Albert Camus. To see his work check out his website: www.jwkash.com or connect with him on Twitter @j_w_kash or Instagram @jwkash.

Ashley Okwuosa is a Nigerian writer and journalist based in New York who will read anything by Jhumpa Lahiri and Chimamanda Ngozi Adichie. Connect with her (and send book recommendations) on Twitter @ashleyokwuosa or email ashleyokwuosa@gmail.com.

Jennifer Nguyen is a New York-based journalist who loves "The Count of Monte Cristo" and other novels from Alexandre Dumas. You can reach her on Twitter at @jennaywins.

Pragya Krishna is a writer from India who wishes she could have met James Baldwin. Reach her at pkrishna524@gmail.com.

Bianca Heyward is a New York-based writer who is currently working a book about the opioid epidemic inspired by the work of Joan Didion, David Carr, and Truman Capote. Connect with her on Twitter @biancaheyward or email bianca.ar.heyward@gmail.com.

Momo Hu is a writer from Shanghai who currently lives in New York who likes Zweig and Murakami among others. Connect with her on Twitter @YimoHu or Email yimo.hu@icloud.com.

Leena Sanzgiri is a New York-based writer and audio producer who loves anything by Jhumpa Lahiri. Connect with her on Twitter @leenasanzgiri or at leenasanzgiri@gmail.com.

Heather Schröering is a journalist and film photographer in New York who credits Ruth Reichl's "Garlic and Sapphires" with teaching her how to write and eat. Follow her on Instagram and Twitter at @OhItsHeather, and email her at heather.schro@gmail.com.

Let us know how you like the book on notwhoipictured@gmail.com.

95314197R00098

Made in the USA
Columbia, SC
08 May 2018